W9-BMV-103

Software Configuration Management

Software Configuration Management

Identification, Accounting, Control, and Management

Steve J. Ayer

Frank S. Patrinostro

McGraw-Hill, Inc.

New York St. Louis San Francisco Auckland Bogotá
Caracas Lisbon London Madrid Mexico Milan
Montreal New Delhi Paris San Juan São Paulo
Singapore Sydney Tokyo Toronto

Library of Congress Cataloging-in-Publication Data

Ayer, Steve J.
Software configuration management : identification, accounting, control, and management / Steve J. Ayer, Frank S. Patrinostro.
p. cm. — (McGraw-Hill software engineering series)
Includes index.
ISBN 0-07-002603-3
1. Software configuration management. I. Patrinostro, Frank S. II. Title. III. Series.
QA76.76.C69A94 1992
005.1'068'4—dc20 92-4519
CIP

1 2 3 4 5 6 7 8 9 0 DOC/DOC 9 7 6 5 4 3 2

ISBN 0-07-002603-3

The sponsoring editor for this book was Jerry Papke, the editing supervisor was Joseph Bertuna, and the production supervisor was Suzanne W. Babeuf. It was set in Century Schoolbook.

Printed and bound by R.R. Donnelley & Sons Company.

Contents

List of Figures and Tables

Preface

This book is intended to integrate the basic theories of configuration management and change control with the design, development, and implementation of computer-based management information systems. Such an integration emphasizes the importance of a systems development methodology (SDM) that breaks the systems life cycle into phases and tasks and identifies the deliverable items of each task. More importantly, it provides insights into how the MIS organizational structure responsible for the development of a computer system can apply technical and administrative direction to ensure that changes to a software configuration are processed in an orderly manner.

This book represents a significant departure from the numerous attempts that have been made to relate traditional engineering concepts of configuration management to the development and control of computer systems. In our judgment, much of the traditional material is essential; however, the unique thrust of software development makes it imperative to correlate the end-item orientation of the system life cycle with any discussion of configuration management and change control. This book is unique because it focuses on defining configuration identification baselines that correlate specifically with the phased development of a computer system.

The primary features of this book are as follows:

- At the outset the characteristics of the MIS environment in which software configuration management practices will be applied are emphasized.
- Project management is related to configuration management in terms of planning, project control, evaluation, change control, and project file management.
- Baselines are defined for maintaining control of changes to a software configuration identification.
- A labeling scheme for identifying the items that comprise a baseline identification is defined.
- Mechanisms for evaluating and approving or disapproving changes to a baseline identification are described and illus-

trated.

- The elements of the change management process from change initiation to installation monitoring are logically related.
- The functions of the change control board (CCB) that oversees maintenance of the information data base are delineated.
- Detailed procedures are provided for recording and reporting information on the status of proposed changes and the implementation of approved changes.
- The auditing function aimed at validating the satisfactory completion of a configuration item is explained and illustrated.

The subject matter of the six chapters has been arranged in what we believe to be a pedagogically sound sequence. Each chapter has a summary, and almost all have examples and illustrations.

The list of colleagues to whom the authors feel a sense of gratitude for ideas and suggestions is too long to enumerate here. With respect to this book; we are particularly grateful to Jerry Papke, senior editor at TAB/McGraw-Hill for making this book a reality.

Suggestions and comments on the text and the related materials are solicited.

Steve J. Ayer
Frank S. Patrinostro

Chapter

1

Overview of the Software Configuration Management Process

1.0 Introduction

The objective of this book is to provide a methodological framework for software development and to define standards for managing the configuration items that comprise the baselines for management and control. In order to understand the role of configuration management in a software development environment, however, one must begin with dissecting the term *software configuration management.*

- *Software,* as defined in this book, includes the programs, procedures, routines, and all documents associated with the analysis, design, programming, conversion, and implementation of a computer system.

- *Configuration,* in a software context, is defined as the aggregate of deliverable items that result from the tasks performed during the phased development of the system. The configuration includes operating system programs used by computer equipment in responding to an application program; data base data that is stored in a form capable of being processed and operated on by a computer; system/subsystem specifications that define performance, organizational, and environmental and interfacing requirements; computer software documentation that explains the capabilities of the software, or provides operating instructions for using or maintaining the software; computer programs that are subject to change; executable programs that are resident in read-only or erasable ROM memory and cannot be readily modified; program code used to translate or convert each operation into a computer-understandable language; support software designed to support the development, maintenance, and modification of other software; utility programs required for the generation of the operational and support programs; test software utilized in the testing of the program code; and computer software library materials that provide proper identification, storage, and protection.

- *Management* of the software configuration environment is defined as the administrative discipline that is exercised to identify and document the functional and physical characteristics of each software configuration item, control changes to those characteristics, record and report change processing and implementation status, and verify and validate software performance and the adequacy and completeness of documentation.

The following might be considered an appropriate definition of software configuration management:

> Software configuration management is the process of exercising administrative surveillance and control of the sum total of computer equipment, computer software, and all associated documentation.

The definition can, of course, be amplified by further describing software configuration management as follows:

> Software configuration management is the process of identifying, tracking, and controlling changes to software configuration items that define needs, evaluate the technical and cost feasibility of the system, and establish the functional requirements; identify specific hardware and software functions to be performed; set forth the design specifications, define the user procedures and controls, and establish plans for implementation and maintenance; transform the design specifications into executable code; establish specifications for testing and reporting on test results; and provide operational documentation, including program packages, user guides, operator manuals, and training materials.

From these definitions, perhaps we can begin to establish a framework for developing a software configuration management methodology. The implementation of a configuration management methodology must be integrated with a systems development methodology and project management methodology to provide a consistent, workable environment for software development, implementation, and control. The following pages outline the concepts of each of these components to management in a software environment.

1.1 Systems Development Methodology

The methodology used for systems development establishes the framework for software configuration identification and baseline management. The *systems development methodology* (SDM) breaks the systems development process into a series of manageable phases. A series of tasks and task steps define each phase. Each task or group of tasks results in one or more definable items that are deliverable to the project file. The aggregate of deliverable items that are cumulated at specified stages of the development process form the baselines for configuration management and change control.

The SDM model will differ from organization to organization, but in most methodologies the process revolves around five major functions of systems development concern:

- Define the functional specifications
- Allocate functional specifications to subsystems
- Prepare design specifications
- Program the design
- Maintain the system.

The approach to systems development that is associated with the configuration management process presented in this book is characterized by breaking down the systems development cycle into nine development phases:

Initial investigation
Feasibility study
Requirements definition
External design
Internal design
Programming
Testing
Conversion
Implementation

1.1.1 Initial Investigation

The methodology begins with an initial investigation phase. The starting point of the initial investigation process is the issuance of a project request submitted by the manager of a user department (e.g., accounting department, purchasing department, sales department, etc.). The information on the project request generally includes a statement of the present system's problems and an explanation as to why a new system is being proposed. When the request is approved, the data processing organization will embark on the development effort. If the request is for a major enhancement to an existing system, an analyst, or a team of analysts, may be assigned the responsibility of conducting an initial investigation to further define the problems and needs identified by the project request. The project request document itself becomes the first item subject to configuration control.

The first task performed by the analysts assigned to conduct the initial investigation is to interview the probable users of the new system. The objective is to acquire a detailed understanding of the existing problems and the goals for the proposed system. The second task is to review the strengths and weaknesses of the proposed system. The third task focuses on developing a feasibility study plan. The final task is the preparation of an initial investigation phase end-document or initial investigation report to document the findings.

1.1.2 Feasibility Study

The tasks to be performed to determine the feasibility of the proposed project are geared to answer three questions: What needs to be done? How can it be done? What is the value of doing it? Expressed somewhat differently, the feasibility study phase of software development provides answers to questions that address the operational, technical, and economic feasibility of developing the proposed system.

The first group of tasks performed focuses on reviewing the present system to gain a thorough understanding of what it does and how it does it. The second group of tasks involves a preliminary analysis of the requirements that the proposed system must meet. The third group of tasks involves the identification of possible development alternatives. The fourth group of tasks focuses on comparing the estimated costs of development and operation to the anticipated benefits. The final task is to prepare a feasibility study phase-end document.

Using the information presented in the feasibility study document, management decides whether or not to proceed with the project.

1.1.3 Requirements Definition

The objective of the requirements definition phase is to transform the user needs defined during the initial investigation and feasibility study phases into specific requirements. The tasks performed during the requirements definition phase are aimed at determining functional requirements, systems requirements, environmental requirements (e.g., equipment), and data requirements. They are also concerned with establishing criteria for the evaluation of vendor packages. During the requirements definition phase, various hardware/software tradeoff studies are performed and operational sequences defined and examined. In addition, the interface requirements and system operating concepts are defined. At the conclusion of this phase a requirements definition phase-end document is published.

1.1.4 External Design

The external design proposes a system model for achieving the system objectives and meeting the specified requirements. It defines the major subsystems and specifies how the system functions are allocated among those subsystems. The first set of tasks performed by the external design team results in documentation that describes the overall software subsystem design concepts and shows how the computer programs fit into the design. The second set of tasks defines the security, privacy, and control functions. The third set of tasks considers the technical environment. The fourth set of tasks focuses on identifying interfaces among the computer programs. The final step is to prepare an external design phase-end document.

1.1.5 Internal Design

During the internal design phase of development, the detailed processing logic is defined, reports and display layouts are prepared, the program and module interfaces are designed, and record and file structures are specified. All the definitions are prepared in very specific and exact terms, and all the specifications necessary for a programmer to code the programs are finalized. The first set of tasks performed by the internal design team focuses on generating detailed descriptions of all inputs and outputs relevant to the system being designed. The second set of tasks is concerned with creating the logical data base design. The third set of tasks performed by the internal design team is aimed at developing program specifications. The fourth set of tasks is concerned with defining procedures for controls, security, backup, and recovery. The final step before preparing the internal design phase-end document is the preparation of plans for the remainder of the development effort. The plans include test plans, conversion plans, implementation plans, maintenance plans, and documentation plans.

1.1.6 Programming

The programming phase of the systems development process involves translating the program specifications into executable code. Coding should be performed in accord with established programming standards. It is extremely important that sufficient comments be written during the coding to permit easy traceability from the program listings to the logic flows. Programming is actually the final phase of the product development effort, although a great deal of work remains to be done in testing, converting, implementing, and maintaining the system to complete the development life cycle.

The document items resulting from the programming phase include program descriptions, source program listings, object listings, cross-reference listings, and routine identifications.

1.1.7 Testing

The testing process involves a series of tasks aimed at ensuring that the coded program satisfies the functional and performance requirements. The documentation prepared as a result of these activities must communicate the test specifications, define evaluation procedures, provide a written record of test results, and analyze performance data.

Although a significant amount of the testing actually takes place during the programming phase, the testing process is considered as a separate phase. It follows the programming phase in the methodology used as a model in this book simply because the actual running of the tests can take place only after the coding is completed. In fact, unit testing is generally performed as soon as the coding of each program module is completed; module integration testing takes place as related modules pass unit test; and verification and acceptance testing are performed only after all the modules have been coded. The overall testing process is controlled by a variety of test documentation. These include test plans, test procedures, and test reports.

1.1.8 Conversion

The conversion phase encompasses those tasks required to convert input files, tables, etc. from existing formats to those required by the new system. The tasks performed during the conversion process focus on file conversion, file creation, and data entry requirements, as well as formalizing strategies for training both user and data processing personnel. The activities of this phase include developing a schedule for system turnover.

1.1.9 Implementation

The implementation phase tasks result in the system being integrated into the normal operational activities of the business. The tasks to be performed include the completion of all file conversions, equipment installations, user guides and desk instructions, training, and security authorizations. Computer operations personnel must also be trained, and operations documentation prepared. Upon system certification, the program files are placed into production, and the system is monitored to ensure successful operation.

1.2 Project Management Methodology

Just as the systems development methodology establishes the framework for software configuration identification and baseline management, the project management methodology establishes the framework for managing changes to the software configuration. The project management approach associated with the configuration management methodology presented in this book views project management responsibilities in terms of five basic functions:

- Planning
- Project control
- Evaluation
- Change control
- Project file management

A series of tasks and task steps exists within each functional area. The methodology prescribes that the results of certain tasks, or groups of tasks, be adequately documented. Since project management is an integral part of the systems development process, the project management methodology must coincide with the methodology that defines the systems development life cycle phases.

1.2.1 Planning

The planning segment of project management should reemphasize the tasks and task steps prescribed by the SDM. Specifically, it should define the work breakdown structure, determine documentation requirements, define standards for project development, and establish milestones for project management and project control. The software development plan should specify the ties with the organization's configuration management plan and incorporate tasks required for configuration identification and control. It should also outline procedures for staffing, estimating, working with subcontractors, and preparing a project plan.

The project manager should ensure that a clearly defined statement of work be formally agreed upon by the data processing organization and the user organization(s) prior to initiation of the project. The statement of work is a narrative description of the work to be performed. It should be specific in defining the objectives to be accomplished, major task deliverables, and the chronological order for delivery. If the project involves a phased delivery over a long span of time (6 months or longer), the statement of work should be specific for each phase.

User commitment to the project and agreement on the statement of work are prerequisites to developing the project plans. The plan should incorporate regular project reviews to ensure ongoing agreement with schedules and deliverables.

The project management methodology should prescribe two levels of project planning - general planning and detail planning. The guidelines concerned with general planning should focus on helping the project manager define the overall scope of work to be performed. The primary results of general planning are an overall budget and a schedule for the effort required and the elapsed time necessary to accomplish each activity. General planning involves identifying the tasks to be performed during each phase of development, evaluating each selected task in terms of the effort required for performance, and identifying the relationships and interdependencies between the tasks. As a part of the general planning process, personnel requirements must be identified in terms of both numbers of people required and the skill requirements for each. Individuals selected to staff the project are then allocated specific tasks based upon availability and capability. The object of detail planning is to refine the estimates and schedules by using task relationships and resource leveling. This activity generally results in a baseline schedule of allocations based on organizational requirements and PERT and/or bar charts that provide management with a tool to plan the allocation of resources. Since labor resources do not always provide the proper capability at the proper time, the project management methodology should suggest guidelines for revising the estimates and schedules at any point during the project life cycle. If subcontractor labor is required, the approach to selecting and managing the work assigned to a subcontractor must be carefully considered.

The final result of the planning process is the development of a project plan that describes how the project manager plans to conduct the software development project. The plan content includes documents that identify the project milestones, define the task deliverables, and specify who reviews the project, when, and for what purpose. It also includes items that identify key personnel and describe how the line and staff organizations associated with the project interface.

Planning is a continuing and iterative process throughout the life of a project. The project control methodology suggests specific types of review throughout the life of the project. Each review point should be a triggering mechanism to the project manager to identify potential schedule slippages or deviations (from standards, design, etc.) in the plan.

1.2.2 Project Control

The project control segment of the project management methodology is concerned with helping project managers to define the procedures for starting a project, tracking and reporting, and reviewing project progress. It involves the continuous assessment of planned versus actual performance. To be effective, at least three conditions must prevail. First, a project plan must exist. Second, the team must know at what level they are performing in relation to the plan. Third, they must know and understand, at all times, the overall objectives of the project and the work to be accomplished in each development phase. The procedures for starting a project establish protocols for reviewing and approving the project plan and obtaining formal sign-offs related to the committed costs and committed dates. The tracking and reporting procedures explain the functions of weekly time reports, work completion reports, computer usage reports, and incident reports. The progress reporting procedures demonstrate the use of PERT, bar (Gantt) charts, and graphics as a means for exhibiting or plotting progress. The procedures for reviewing project progress provide guidance for conducting peer reviews, periodic reviews, milestone reviews, and phase reviews. They also provide guidance for preparing reports that document the findings and recommendations of each of the review teams. Figure 1-1 illustrates the planning, control, and evaluation for the life cycle of a software development project.

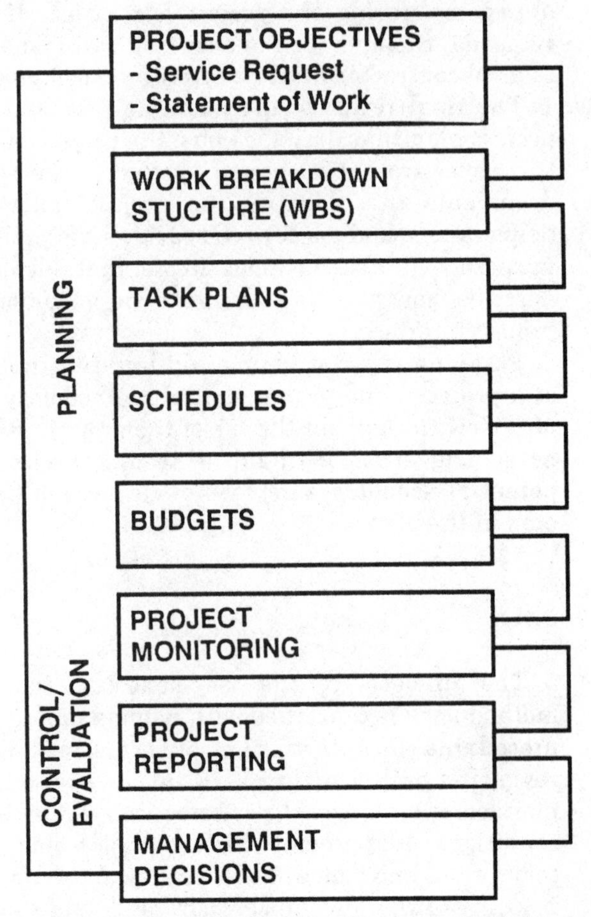

Figure 1-1. Project Planning, Control, and Evaluation.

The project control process should provide for the continuous assessment of planned versus actual performance. Effective project control mandates that a project plan exist and that the project team know and understand the overall project direction. Control is accomplished only when a project activity can be posted against the project plan and progress can be measured in terms of schedule and resource utilization. At the conclusion of each reporting activity, the PERT and/or bar charts that plot schedules and resource allocations must be rescheduled and updated to reflect the actual circumstances applied to the reported resource allocation.

To properly control a project, the schedule for completion of tasks and activities should be periodically reviewed and updated with changes and accomplishments. If the project review reveals activities that are behind schedule, a decision must be made to increase phase resources to get the project back on schedule or to allow the schedule to be delayed. The project manager should carefully analyze the schedule and the resources assigned to ensure that the expected level of performance is being achieved. The project manager may consider several questions in the analysis:

Are the tasks more complex than originally anticipated?

Do the individuals assigned to the task have the skill levels, experience, training, etc. to perform the tasks assigned?

Is there a bottleneck in the flow of information or procedures on the project, either to or from users to the project manager, project manager to analyst, user to analyst, analyst to programmer, systems development to computer operations or vice versa?

Are there unanticipated hardware or software problems?

There is always potential for falling behind schedule due to any number of reasons. If the project manager uses the tools available and includes the use of those tools during the planning phase, that potential becomes greatly diminished. Reviewing schedules only at the end of a reporting period will certainly reveal whether the project is on or off schedule. However, it places the project manager in a defensive position. This may be avoided entirely if the project manager will insist upon and enforce the use of each of the following project reviews.

The peer review, which is conducted for each critical task of the project, becomes the first line of defense in detecting errors that may ultimately cause schedule delays or unmet project objectives.

The periodic review is used to determine project status, identify problem areas, and to report progress to the project team.

Milestone reviews are a communication vehicle between the development and user communities to report and review performance and project status.

Phase reviews should be sponsored by and comprised of upper-level management from the development and user organizations as well as quality assurance representatives. The phase review is essential to validate objectives and progress status upon completion of a project development phase.

Each review should be incorporated into the project schedule and task plans. Many of the reviews will be done by different people and there may be overlap in the reviews depending on the type of review conducted. In any event, each review must be thoroughly documented and immediately followed up with any remedial action necessary to correct deficiencies. In many cases the project manager will be delegating responsibility for the corrective actions. Figure 1-2 illustrates the review process and how it can become intermingled.

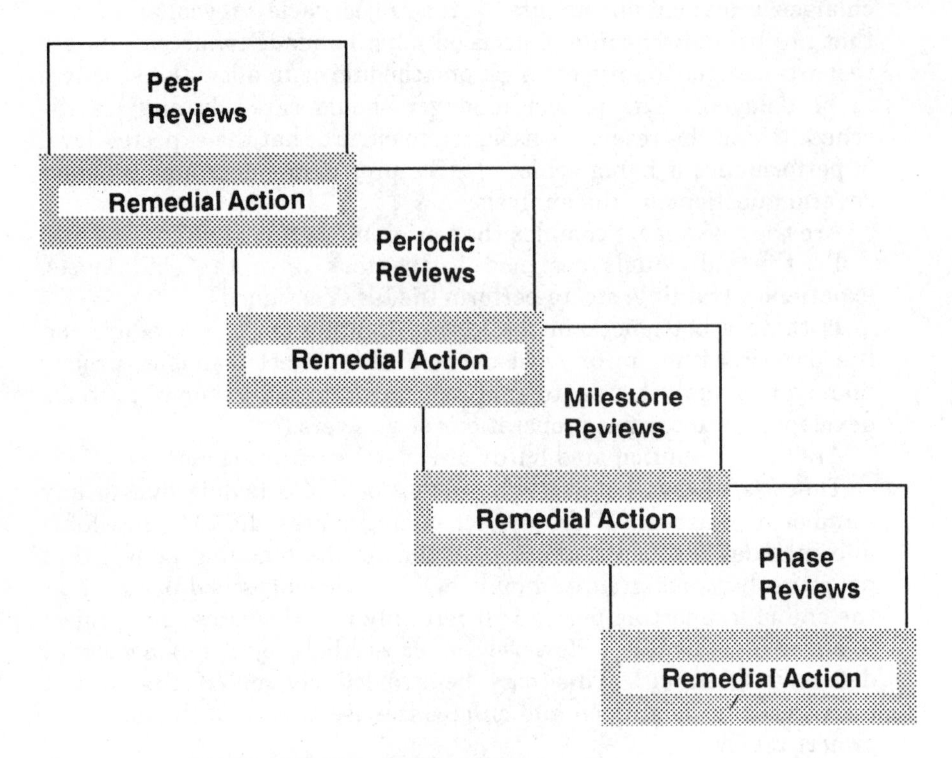

Figure 1-2. The Project Review Process.

The monitoring of schedules for small projects can usually be satisfied with manual methods such as Gantt charts. More complex projects, however, may require the development and/or implementation of a computer-based tracking system. There are a number of automated project scheduling and tracking systems that are either personal computer or mainframe computer based. Which is best for a particular project depends on the size and complexity of the project at hand. Some of the PC based tools available today are quite sophisticated.

1.2.3 Evaluating

The evaluating segment of the project management methodology should be aimed at helping a project manager define procedures for evaluating both the product and project. It provides guidelines for performing a cost/benefit analysis and a risk analysis. The cost/benefit analysis methodology provides task guidelines for identifying and assessing tangible and intangible benefits, evaluating development and recurring costs, and assessing the value of the project to the organization. The risk analysis methodology defines procedures for analyzing both product risks and project risks.

The cost analysis process involves studying cost reports and other operating cost data to determine if cost reductions can be achieved (e.g., reductions in the cost of repairs and maintenance, machine rentals, and staff expense). The benefits analysis process is primarily concerned with evaluating tangible and intangible benefits and quantifying objectives (e.g., reductions in personnel, improved service, etc.). In assessing the benefits of a project, it is often necessary to calculate the payback period and the return on investment. The tradeoffs associated with each alternative should also be identified and assessed. When cost/benefits are concluded, the two factors should be interrelated to assess the overall value of the project.

Risk analysis is another ongoing responsibility of the project manager. The process of analyzing risk involves three separate functions. They are duration risk analysis, product risk analysis, and project risk analysis.

Duration risk analysis focuses on determining the impact of delayed schedules. In some organizations, the risk associated with delayed schedules may not be crucial. In others, delays can result in great losses.

Product risk analysis is concerned with evaluating the risk of producing a deficient product (e.g., the impact of limited resources on quality assurance).

Project risk analysis is aimed at evaluating the overall capability of the organization to accomplish the desired results in a timely manner and within budget constraints.

1.2.4 Change Control

The change control segment of the change management methodology must concern itself with establishing procedures for two categories of change - product changes and project changes. The procedures for product change control must be coordinated with those elements of the configuration management plan that define the configuration identification, control, accounting, and auditing requirements and must establish the policies and procedures for controlling changes to source code, load modules, procedures, parameters, JCL, macros, screen maps, copylibs, test procedures, test data, and documentation. The procedures for project change must be coordinated with those elements of the plan that define the roles and responsibilities of each unit in the organization that is involved in the project. Thus, procedures for both product change and product change must be consistent with the configuration management plan.

Configuration control for some projects may require separate environments for development, test, quality assurance, training, and production. These multiple versions must all originate from some baseline for each environment which represents a starting point of a static or frozen version (see Figure 1-3).

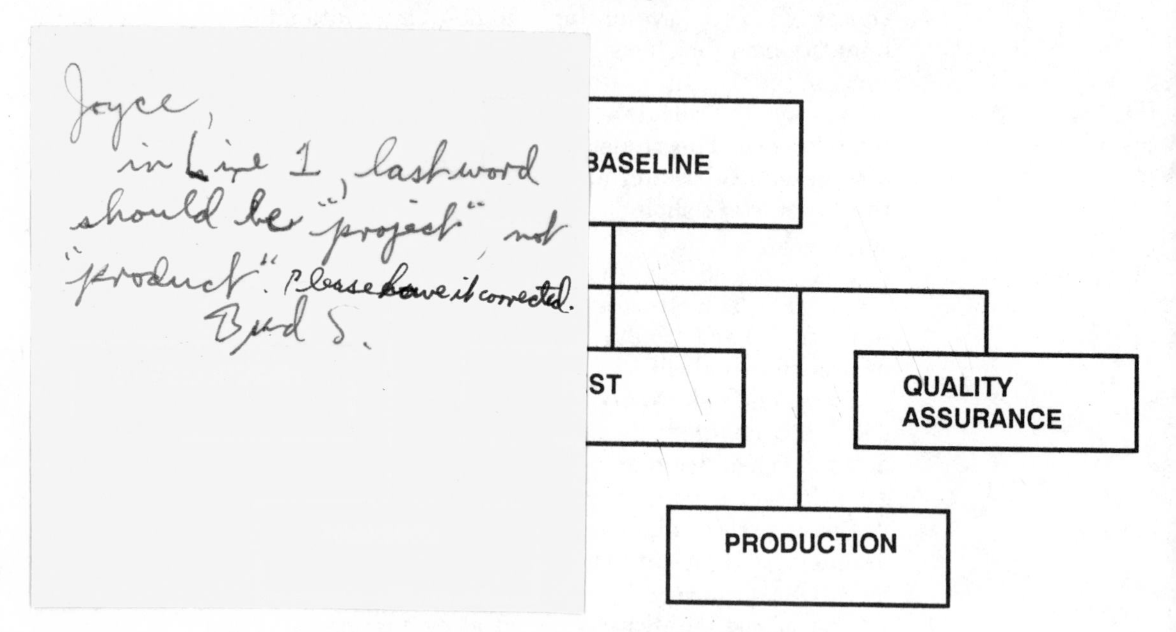

Figure 1-3. Development Baselines.

Controlling the configuration and changes may be a full-time position for one of the team members; if the project is very large, the allocation of this position is advised.

Without adequate controls the impact of changes may create serious problems and costly overruns. Some of these consequences may include:

- Changes that are unidentifiable
- Changes that are very difficult and/or costly to remove
- Changes that are not properly documented
- Changes to the wrong versions of software
- Unauthorized changes that may result in financial loss to the company
- Conflicts during conversion, implementation, or during parallel operations
- Complete loss of project control

The first step in the change management process is to define policy to control the manner in which changes are introduced and processed. Policy should be written and published for each element of the following elements that comprise the change management process :

- Change initiation
- Technical assessment
- Business assessment
- Management approval
- Test tracking
- Installation tracking

Figure 1-4 illustrates the change management elements for which policy should be established.

CMM

Element	Policy objective
Change Initiation	To establish a consistent approach to initiating change requests
Technical Assessment	To promote and ensure technical completeness and installability of proposed changes
Business Assessment	To support the establishment of procedures for approving changes
Management Approval	To establsh procedures for approving/disapproving or delaying proposed changes to configure items
Test Tracking	To ensure that the testing process adheres to testing standards and schedules
Installation Tracking	To monitor the effectiveness of the installation process

Figure 1-4. Change Management Policies.

Change Initiation Policy. The development of a change initiation policy involves defining the types of changes to be controlled and the functions of a change control board (CCB). A change control board makes visible the impact of requested changes, from both a technical and a business assessment, on the project objectives and schedules. Further, the responsibility for approval or disapproval does not rest solely with the project manager or the data processing manager, and the requestor must justify the need for the change.

Technical Assessment Policy. The technical assessment policy defines the process for evaluating the technical merit of a proposed change.

Business Assessment Policy. The business assessment policy addresses the impact the change will have on the business goals and ensures that the timing of the proposed change is compatible with those goals. The topics covered may include categories and/or types of changes, change request methods, procedures; performance indicators, tracking status of change requests, authorized approvers, and change coordination responsibilities.

Management Approval Policy. The management approval policy focuses on providing management with a basis for evaluating the recommendations resulting from the technical and business assessments and approving or disapproving a requested change.

Test Tracking Policy. The test tracking policy emphasizes topics such as test levels, reporting procedures, responsibilities for testing, and performance indicators. It establishes the framework for monitoring test results to ensure that changes are tested in a consistent manner.

Installation Tracking Policy. The installation tracking policy is established to ensure that the installation of the change adheres to set standards, change plans, and procedures. The topics generally considered in defining installation tracking policy include change schedules (daily, weekly, etc.) and concurrent changes in the hardware and software environments.

In addition to the six elements discussed in the preceding paragraphs, policy should be defined that provides for central direction and monitoring of all proposed changes to established configuration baselines. The coordinating activity generally takes the form of a change control board (CCB) that bears the responsibility for the overall effectiveness of change management. The basic activities of the coordinating activity are to review change requests for completeness, verify that change requests are properly entered into the data base, and enforce policies and procedures.

1.2.5 Project File

The project file segment of the project management methodology should combine the functions of a technical reference library, a systems documentation library, and a program maintenance library. It should provide guidance for defining functions relative to acquisitions, cataloging, organization, circulation, and disposition.

The acquisition methodology divides the acquisition process into two sub-functions: acquisition of internally generated documents and acquisition of externally generated documents.

The cataloging methodology focuses on procedures for descriptive cataloging, classifying project file items, and preparing indexes to enable the user to locate important items registered in the project file.

The organization methodology discusses the various devices and filing methods required to accommodate the variety of media to be entered into the project file.

The circulation methodology explains the functions of an authorized patron file, title file, in-circulation file, and hold file.

The disposition methodology provides alternatives for continued maintenance of the project file when the project is completed.

1.3 Configuration Management Methodology

The term *configuration management methodology* is used in this book to identify the discipline of applying technical and administrative direction and surveillance to a software development project. The application of configuration management involves four basic elements:

- Configuration identification, which focuses on identifying the items of a software system that are subject to change during the life cycle of a project
- Configuration change control, which enables the systematic evaluation, coordination, approval or disapproval, and implementation of all approved changes to configuration items
- Configuration status accounting, which provides a mechanism for administrative tracking and reporting of all software items identified and controlled
- Configuration auditing, which serves to verify and validate the software configuration

The successful implementation of each configuration management element is contingent, to a large extent, on the preparation of formal documentation for the purpose of:

- Defining baseline components and maintaining control of changes to the components
- Communicating, coordinating, scheduling, monitoring, and controlling changes to configuration items
- Maintaining records of the system evolution and current status
- Verifying and validating configuration items

The aggregate of configuration management documents is used by the software development team, QA managers, and EDP auditors to ensure consistent quality of work and provide a checkpoint for management decisions.

1.3.1 Configuration Identification

The task of configuration identification is to uniquely identify each component item of a software system. This unique identification enables the software organization to accurately track and control software changes, multiple versions of a software product, and multiple software products. The key concept in configuration identification in a development environment is the configuration baseline. A *baseline* is defined as a configuration identification document, or set of documents, prepared at a specified milestone in the software development process. Baselines can be established at any milestone in the software development cycle where it is deemed necessary to define a point for control of future changes in performance and design. The baselines, once established, constitute the configuration identification. Figure 1-5 illustrates a set of baseline documents, indicating the function of each document.

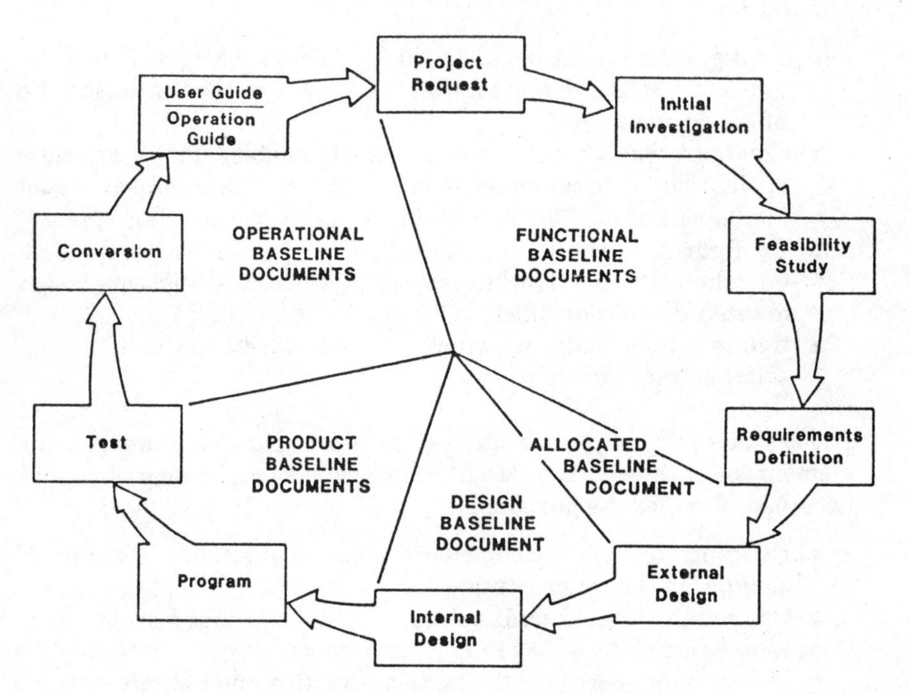

Figure 1-5. Baseline Documents of the Software Development Life Cycle.

The configuration management methodology presented here is based on five categories of baseline documents:

- Functional baseline documents that describe the problem, establish preliminary costs and target schedules, and define the functional requirements
- Allocated baseline documents that establish a baseline for determining what has to be done to bring the system into being and what will be achieved by installing it
- Design baseline documents that define system constraints and set forth the program design specifications that programmers will need to code programs
- Product baseline documents that provide a complete description of all computer subprogram functions and structures
- Operational baseline documents that consist of validated components of a tested program

The specific document types that comprise each category are shown in Figure 1-6.

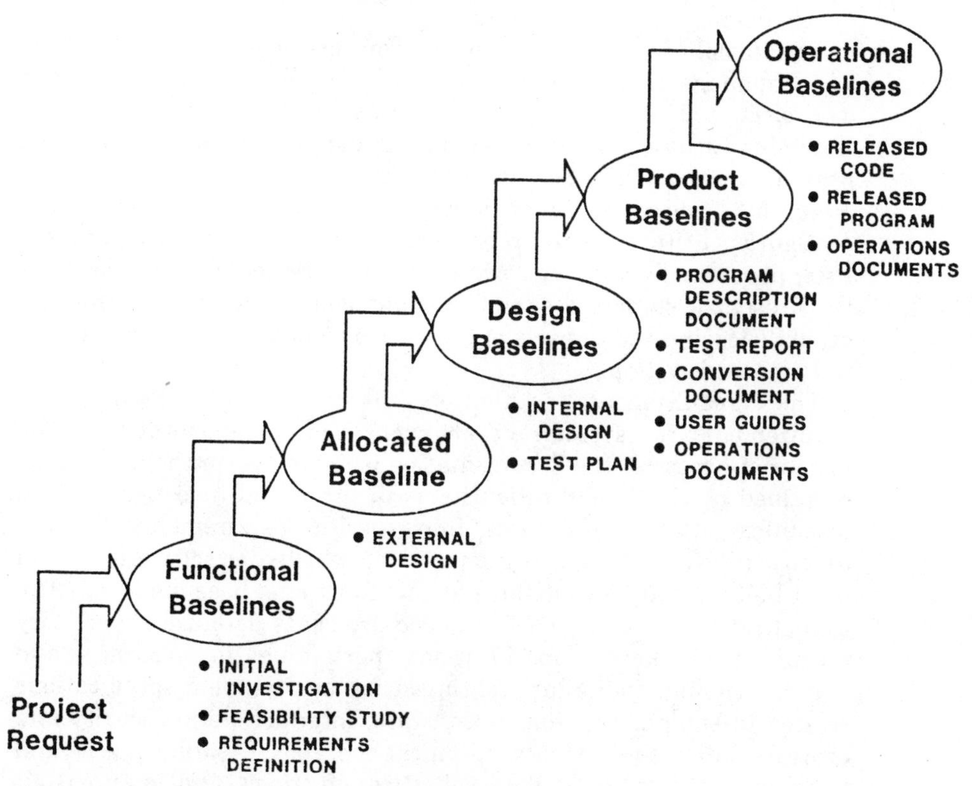

Figure 1-6. Categories of Baseline Documents.

Functional Baseline. There are three levels of the functional baseline in the software development cycle discussed in this book.

- Initial investigation baseline
- Feasibility study baseline
- Requirements definition baseline

The initial investigation documentation delivered to the project file defines the first level of the functional baseline. It allows management to estimate the potential of a new system in terms of cost and benefits and serves as a vehicle for analyzing requirements and assessing the technical and economic impact of implementing the new system. It also enables management to determine the nature of the existing problem, conceive an adequate solution, and project schedules for development. The collection of software configuration items delivered to the initial investigation repository includes statements that explain existing problems and needs for a new system, preliminary cost proposals for each phase of development, and target schedules for starting and completing each phase of development.

The feasibility study documentation provides a baseline from which management can decide whether to undertake development of a project. The software configuration items contained in the feasibility study repository enable management to compare the present system with the proposed system and to identify probable costs and consequences of investing in the new system. The configuration items in the repository include schematics, equipment lists, program listings, etc., which summarize the characteristics of the present system and summary statements which review the new capabilities and the impacts of the various additions/ modifications of the proposed system.

The requirements definition documentation details the requirements for systems development and implementation. The primary purpose of the documentation is to transform the user needs described by the configuration items in the initial investigation and feasibility study repositories into specific requirements for the proposed system. The requirements for which the software system must be tested are also defined at this functional baseline level. The configuration items stored in the requirements definition repository include performance specifications pertaining to accuracy and validity, timing, and failure contingencies; environment specifications related to equipment, support software, interfaces, and security and control; data requirements specifications that describe static and dynamic data elements, data collection functions, and input/output formats; and criteria to be used in selecting vendor software.

Allocated Baseline. The allocated baseline for configuration control is established by the documentation contained in the external design repository. These configuration items provide the design team with a baseline for developing the internal design. The configuration items stored in the external design repository may include descriptions of inputs and outputs, the technical environment in which the system will operate, and definitions of the interfacing functions.

Design Baseline. The documentation stemming from the tasks performed during the internal design establishes the baseline for controlling changes to all *software configuration items* (SCIs) that define the system architecture, data structures, and data base specifications. The configuration items in the design baseline repository define system constraints, provide guidelines for control and security, and set forth the program design specifications that programmers will need to code programs. The program test plan delivered to the project file during the internal design phase of software development defines the total scope of the testing to be performed and identifies the particular level of testing to be performed.

Product Baseline. The documents that establish the product baseline for configuration management include:

- Program description documentation
- Test reports
- Conversion documentation
- User guide
- Operations guide

The program description documentation in the product baseline repository provides a complete technical description of all computer subprogram functions, structures, operation environments, operating constraints, data base organization, source and object code listing, and diagrammatic/narrative flows.

The test reports contained in the repository provide a vehicle to convey results of required tests. They are used to describe, define, and evaluate discrepancies between the intended system or program design and the program capability as produced in code.

The conversion documents delivered to the project file establish the baseline for converting and controlling new files and updating existing files.

The user guide provides the organization's non-EDP personnel with the information necessary to effectively use the system. The configuration items presented in a user guide include display screens for specific input/output and instructions for user interactions; document content descriptions; and explanations of reports to be generated by the system.

The operations guide documentation includes descriptions of operations requirements for security and privacy; instructions for running jobs; explanations of messages that may occur during the running of a job; procedures for aborting and restarting the system; and definitions of backup procedures and file retention requirements.

Operational Baseline. The operational baseline consists of the validated components of a tested program. The baseline is established when the testing process is completed and certified as ready for release for integration with other system elements. Once this baseline is established, changes to the product baseline documents must be processed through formal configuration control channels.

The first four types of baselines (i.e., functional, allocated, design, and product baselines) take the form of physical documentation that records the results of tasks performed during each phase of the software development cycle. The operational baseline, on the other hand, is the actual program code resulting from the released product baseline.

1.3.2 Configuration Control

Configuration control documents provide an administrative mechanism for evaluating and approving or disapproving proposed changes to a software system. There are several types of control documents. These include:

- Change control documents
- Corporate policies
- Operating procedures
- Document control forms
- Standards and guidelines

The functions of the various control documents are summarized below. Step-by-step instructions for the preparation of the various document types are provided in Chapter 4.

Change Control Documents. The document types associated with configuration change control are:

- Change classification index
- Change request (CR)
- Change action report (CAR)
- Discrepancy report (DR)
- Discrepancy action report (DAR)
- Status report

The *change classification index* is used to classify changes which impact the approved functional, allocated, design, product, and operational baselines.

The *change request* proposes a change to an existing requirement or limitation of the system. The CR may be initiated by anyone and submitted through approved channels to the change control board.

The *change action report* is the release document for a CR and serves to record and disseminate change control board action or disposition. It may also serve as the release form for any supporting reports or studies required by the change control board to make a proper and informed determination.

The *discrepancy report* reports a discrepancy between system design documents, or between the design documents and a program. It contains information on the discrepancy, such as criticality, recommended priority for change, and any proposed solution or corrective action taken. The DR is submitted through formal channels prior to completion of the system installation to the change control board for approval, disapproval, or conversion to a CR.

The *discrepancy action report* is the release document for a DR. It serves to record the action or disposition taken on a discrepancy report. The discrepancy action report contains specific correction instructions for documentation and programs, together with amplifying information such as the analysis of the discrepancy. The report specifies whether a DR becomes a CR.

The *status report* provides the change control board with status information on approved change requests until completion of the system installation.

Policies. Company policies issued by top management provide a vital measure for configuration control. Policies should be established for:

- Defining and planning software development baselines
- Documenting the configuration items
- Defining the composition of the change control board
- Defining documenting change system procedures
- Defining procedures for processing requests for waivers or deviations from standards

The first step in fulfilling the communications required for effective configuration control is to write policy statements related to the above topics and publish them in a formal software development policy manual.

Operating Procedures. Company policies serve as the vehicle to convey configuration management objectives, but it is in the context of procedures through which these policies are executed. Many organizations combine these two types of documents and publish them in a manual entitled *Policies and Procedures*. The manual can be used to document all the procedures that impact configuration management. Operating procedures should be prepared covering all areas of configuration management. Such operating procedures may include:

- Service request procedures that establish control and accountability from project initiation through resolution
- Incident report procedures that provide instructions for reporting on any type of problem related to a production system
- Forms design and control procedures that establish standards for the design and control of all forms used in the software development process

In a very practical sense, the full effectiveness of configuration management can be realized only to the extent that orderly, efficient procedures are developed through which static plans and policies can be converted into action.

Document Control Forms. Various control forms may be required for effective document control. These include:

- Sign-off sheet
- Change control grid
- Document review control form
- Revision control form

The sign-off sheet should be designed to include the name of the system, release date, signatures of approvers, and a preparer statement.

The change control grid is used to maintain an up-to-date record of changes. As revisions are received and filed in the document, the appropriate revision number is crossed off on the control grid.

The document review control form serves as a document log to control the review process.

The revision control form instructs the document holder as to which pages to remove from the existing document and indicates new pages to be added.

Standards and Guidelines. Having defined the policies and procedures for configuration control, we can now focus on defining standards that promote the consistency of approach in the configuration management process. To facilitate this objective, the standards should be organized and publishes in a configuration management standards manual. Standards establish uniform configuration management practices that can be tailored to all software systems and configuration items. The topics that should be considered in developing standards are described below.

Configuration management plan standards provide criteria to be followed in the implementation of configuration management requirements.

Interface control standards set forth criteria and provide general guidance for the establishment of interface control, including installation requirements.

Specification maintenance standards provide instructions for the preparation of change requests, change action reports, and documentation changes.

Document and item identification numbering and marking standards establish the numbering and identification schemes required to achieve configuration traceability of configuration items.

Release and integration standards establish the minimum requirements for achieving a proper relationship between development specification data and the product and operational baseline configuration items.

Software allocation document standards set forth the criteria to be followed in the development of a software allocation baseline that identifies the allocation of functions between the hardware and software items which comprise the system.

Configuration audit standards set forth the objectives to be accomplished at each of the configuration audits and provide general guidance for the conduct of these audits.

Software change standards provide uniform procedures for preparing, formatting, and processing changes to computer program configuration items.

1.3.3 Configuration Accounting

Software configuration accounting provides a means of recording and reporting information on the status of proposed changes and the implementation of approved changes. Status accounting logs and reports are maintained both for administrative purposes and for reporting configuration item status to project personnel and the user organization. Administrative records include:

- Product logs that list and describe tapes, decks, and source listings of released software routines
- Routine logs that provide an historical record of the development of each software routine
- Software problem report logs that list and describe the problems reported to date
- Software modification report logs that list and describe all modifications made to the configuration identification to date
- Design problem report logs that list and describe all design problems reported by the user or development personnel
- Document revision logs that describe changes made to documentation
- Software change logs that list all software change requests and their disposition
- Data base change logs that list and describe all changes made to the data base
- Site installation logs that identify each site where the software is installed and the software version installed at that site

The reports prepared to convey information on the status of a configuration item to project personnel and software users include:

- A computer program configuration item index that provides a current status of specifications and selected additional documents which summarize the status of a configuration item
- Software status reports that provide information on the status of proposed changes and the implementation status of approved changes
- Data base configuration reports that provide information on the status of the current configuration of the data base
- Version description documents that describe the content and capability of each delivered version of the software system

In summary, a variety of logs and reports may be used for status accounting of configuration items. These documents provide the means of tracking the development and distribution of all configuration items. Not all tracking, of course, may be accomplished through formal logs and reports. In some instances, telephone conversations or audit checks may suffice. In any case, tracking of the configuration status must be accomplished. The preparation of documents applicable to configuration accounting is discussed and illustrated in Chapter 5.

1.3.4 Configuration Audit

Configuration audit documents fall into two categories: *functional configuration audit documents* and *physical configuration audit documents.*

Functional configuration audit documents provide a means of validating the satisfactory completion of a configuration item. The documentation associated with functional auditing ensures that

- Test/analysis data exists for a configuration item, verifying that the item has achieved the performance specified in its functional or design configuration identification
- The project team maintains internal technical documentation that describes the physical configuration of each unit of the configuration item for which test/analysis data is verified

The documentation associated with physical configuration auditing provide guidance for:

- Establishing the product configuration identification
- Selecting configuration items for the audit
- Identifying any differences between the physical configuration of the selected item and the development baseline item(s)
- Certifying that these differences do not degrade the functional characteristics of the selected unit

1.4 Summary

The methodology used for systems development establishes the framework for software configuration management. The development of a computer system evolves through several phases between the time an idea to create a new system is conceived and the time a computer program can produce the system output. Various types of documents are prepared during the development cycle.

Documents produced during the *initial investigation* phase address the potential of the proposed system relative to costs and benefits. Those produced during the *feasibility study* phase compare the present system to the proposed system and identify probable costs and consequences. *Requirements definition* documents establish the functional requirements for the proposed system. Collectively, these documents define the *functional baseline* for configuration management.

The document items produced during the *external design* of software development define the subsystems to which the functional requirements are allocated. They identify the subsystem interfaces and allocate operational priorities related to organizational constraints, technical environment, and security and control. These documents form the *allocated baseline* for software configuration management.

Internal design specifications spell out exactly how the system will be implemented. Documents are produced that establish specifications for designing the data bases, master files, and work files; specify how hardware/software configurations are transformed into technical requirements; explain how to modify software packages; and provide the specifications programmers need to code the programs. Collectively, these documents define the *design baseline* for configuration management.

Program and test documentation provides the information necessary for program coding, debugging, delivery, and maintenance. The documents delivered to the project file during these phases of development establish the *product baseline* for configuration control.

The validated components of a tested program define the *operational baseline* for software configuration management. Once this baseline is established, changes to the product baseline documents must be processed through formal control channels.

The various baselines that establish the configuration identification must be placed under strict control. Any changes to these baselines must adhere to established policies, standards, and guidelines. The status of proposed changes and the implementation of approved changes must be reported to both project personnel and the user organizations, and all changes must be audited and validated prior to release.

Chapter

2

Software Configuration Management Plan

The *software configuration management plan* (SCMP) is a document that defines the policies and procedures to be followed in exercising administrative surveillance in identifying, tracking, and controlling changes to software configuration items. Specifically, the plan establishes standards for:

1. Identifying configuration items that are subject to change during the life cycle of a software project
2. The systematic evaluation, coordination, approval or disapproval, and implementation of all approved changes to configuration items
3. Administrative tracking and reporting of all software items identified and controlled
4. Verifying and validating the software configuration

It also identifies the organizational levels of software development control, as well as their authority and responsibility in the implementation of configuration management. The plan is applicable to all persons in the user and development organizations involved in a systems development effort, as well as contractor organizations responsible for any element of the development activities.

2.1 Content Outline

The content of a configuration management plan should describe all the major features and objectives of configuration management. The essential elements of the software configuration management plan are outlined below and described and illustrated in subsequent paragraphs.

SOFTWARE CONFIGURATION MANAGEMENT PLAN
TABLE OF CONTENTS

4.4.2 Change Control Grid
4.4.3 Document Review Control Form
4.4.4 Revision Control Form
4.5 Standards and Guidelines
4.5.1 Interface Control Standards
4.5.2 Release Requirements Standards

SECTION 5. CONFIGURATION STATUS ACCOUNTING

5.1 Logs
5.1.1 Data Base Change Request Log
5.1.2 Design Problem Report Log
5.1.3 Document Update Transmittal Log
5.1.4 Product Log
5.1.5 Routine Log
5.1.6 Site Installation Log
5.1.7 Software Change Proposal Log
5.1.8 Software Modification Report Log
5.1.9 Software Problem Report Log
5.1.10 Specification Change Notice Log
5.1.11 Test Status Log
5.2 Reports
5.2.1 Change Request Status Summary
5.2.2 Computer Program Inventory Report
5.2.3 Computer Program Library Transmittal Summary
5.2.4 Software Modification Report Summary
5.2.5 Software Problem Report Summary
5.2.6 Test Status Summary Report
5.3 Version Description Documents

SECTION 6. SOFTWARE CONFIGURATION AUDITING

6.1 Functional Configuration Audit
6.1.1 FCA Checklists
6.1.2 Questionnaires
6.1.3 Worksheets
6.1.4 Interview Summary
6.1.5 FCA Verification Form
6.2 Physical Configuration Audit
6.2.1 Design Documentation Checklist
6.2.2 Test Documentation Checklist
6.2.3 Version Description Documentation Checklist
6.2.4 Change Control Documentation Checklist
6.3 Formal Qualification Review

2.2 Content Development Guidelines

Summary guidelines for the sectional development of a software configuration management plan are presented below and on the following pages.

Section 1. GENERAL

1.1 Purpose of the Plan

This subsection should describe the purpose of the document.

Example:

The purpose of this *software configuration management plan (SCMP)* is to establish and document the requirements, standard practices, and procedures for configuration management of software items. Specifically, the document provides:

- Informative data to give you a common understanding of all activities related to configuration management
- Descriptions of the organizational entities responsible for the administration and coordination of the configuration management system
- Requirements for labeling configuration items and defining the configuration baselines
- Policies for change initiation, assessment, management approval, test tracking, and installation tracking
- Instructions for classifying changes, submitting change requests, and preparing change action reports
- Guidelines for recording and reporting of the information that is needed to manage configuration effectively
- Procedures for auditing the functional and physical configuration and conducting formal qualification reviews prior to release
- Forms to aid in the preparation of documentation required for the effective administration and surveillance of changes to software items

---

1.2 Applicable Documentation

The categories of documents that are subject to configuration management are:

- Planning and management documents
- Systems development documentation
- Vendor documents
- Technical memoranda

1.2.1 Planning and Management Documents

Planning and management documents provide the primary means of communications between the configuration management group and those responsible for software development. This paragraph should identify and describe the types of planning and management documents that are subject to configuration control.

Example:

The following planning and management documents are subject to configuration control:

- Software policy manuals that establish the framework for the software development process.
- Software development guidelines that ensure that the policy objectives can be met through strategic planning.
- Systems and programming standards related to naming conventions, data base development, program design, and job flows.
- Procedures that explain what, by whom, and when the work will be performed.

1.2.2 Systems Development Documents

This paragraph should identify and summarize the various documents produced during the system life cycle that are subject to configuration management.

Example:

During the design and release of a software product, various document items are prepared that are subject to configuration management, including:

- Analysis documentation that provides the economic, operational, and technical information management needs to make decisions on the initial feasibility of a project request.
- Design specifications that establish the criteria for software design relative to inputs and outputs, security and control, performance characteristics, and interfacing requirements.
- Program documentation, including program performance specifications, program design specifications, program descriptions, program listings, and subprogram flow charts.
- Test documentation, including test plans, test specifications, test procedures, and test reports.
- Implementation documentation, including user guides, operations guides, and training materials.

1.2.3 Vendor Documents

This paragraph should identify and summarize the various vendor documents that are prepared in support of the development effort or describe the software and hardware configuration for the system and which are subject to configuration management.

Example:

During the design and release of a software product, various vendor documents are acquired which are subject to configuration management, including:

- Operating system documentation that defines installation parameters, explains operating procedures, and provides explanations of the software functions, capabilities, and limitations
- Utility documentation that explains how various software utilities function and defines their various parameters
- Data base management system documentation that describes the interface between the language in which the application is prepared and the data base
- Hardware documentation that defines the limits and function of the computer system and peripheral hardware

---

1.2.4 Technical Memoranda

This paragraph should identify and summarize all technical memoranda subject to configuration management.

Example:

All documents and other written communications that impact the software development process are subject to configuration control, including:

- Letters that discuss administrative details about the project
- Requests for proposals (RFPs) for available software
- Vendor proposals received in response to the RFPs
- Vendor contracts that specify the work breakdown structure of vendor provided services
- Informal memos that discuss technical matters about the project for which a formal concurrence between the development and configuration management groups is necessary
- Formal memos that are officially concurred upon and signed by the development and user management

---

1.3 Definitions

This subsection should provide a listing of any terms, definitions, or acronyms unique to this document and subject to interpretation by the user of the document.

Example:

Baseline
The aggregate of configuration items for a particular stage of development that establishes the configuration identification of the software at that point in the development cycle

Configuration control board
The organizational entity that provides a central control point for the configuration management system

Configuration item
A deliverable that results from the task end-item orientation of the systems development methodology

---

Section 2. CHANGE COORDINATION

The change coordination activities provide central direction for managing changes to configuration items. This section should identify each coordinating activity involved in the administration of the change process.

2.1 Change Control Board

This subsection should include a chart showing the composition of the change control board (CCB) and explain the functions of the board.

2.1.1 Composition of the Change Control Board

This subsection should define the composition of the change control board.

Example:

A change control board (CCB) shall be established that consists of a Chairperson, permanent advisory representatives, and observers.

- Chairperson. The project leader shall act as chairperson. The chairperson shall have full authority to approve or disapprove proposed changes, to establish items for consideration, and to schedule approved changes.

- Permanent representatives. The advisory representatives shall provide information, advice, and recommendations to the chairperson.

- Observers. The chairperson may, at his/her discretion, invite observers to attend and participate in any Change Control meeting.

2.1.2 Functions of the Change Control Board

This subsection should define the composition and explain the functions of the change control board.

Example:

The CCB should adopt operation procedures and guidelines to:

- Promptly process change requests
- Promptly evaluate and act upon discrepancy reports submitted to the board for action
- Establish response time requirements and priorities for all action items
- Provide cost and technical review and approval procedures
- Establish reporting requirements
- Establish scheduling requirements
- Publish status reports as required
- Provide for such other activities and procedures as may be required

2.2 Librarian

This subsection should describe the duties and functions of the software librarian.

Example:

The software librarian shall maintain and control:

- All master copies of configuration baseline items
- Routines used throughout the program
- Records of users of common routines
- Current and historical versions of the programs under development

2.3 Configuration Management Relationship to Project Management

Configuration management and project management are separate functions and sometimes tend to overlap if there is inadequate coordination. This subsection should distinguish between those activities so that the configuration management and project management teams can complement one another.

Example:

The separate functions of project management and configuration management shall be defined as follows:

- *Project management* shall focus on the justification and control of maintenance activities that may consume company resources. *Change management* shall focus on evaluating and ensuring the readiness of a software product before it is released to production.

- *Project management* shall direct all significant development and/or maintenance work. *Change management* shall be responsible for controlling the entry of changes into the production environment.

- *Project management* shall provide periodic checkpoints during the software development cycle to reassess the expected return on investment. *Change management's* only financial concern is the cost of installing the change.

Section 3. SOFTWARE CONFIGURATION IDENTIFICATION

Configuration identification should be established for every configuration item. Initially, the configuration identification establishes the functional requirements. These are later translated into allocated, design, product, and operational baselines.

3.1 Identification Labeling Scheme

This subsection should present the software configuration item labeling scheme. The labeling elements to be considered include project identification baseline identification, phase identification, and subphase identification. The configuration items at each level may be further broken down to identify elements of the identification.

Example:

Each software item stored in the baseline repository must be labeled so that the item can be readily identified. The alphanumeric labeling elements of the item identification are:

1st Element = project identification
2d Element = baseline identification
3d Element = phase identification
4th Element = subphase identification
5th Element = 1st level baseline item
6th Element = 2nd level baseline item
7th Element = 3rd level baseline item
8th Element = 4th level baseline item

The labeling scheme may be expanded to include the following media identifications:

DO = Document
TP = Tape
DI = Disks
PC = Program Code
JC = JCL

3.2 Software Configuration Baseline

This subsection should designate the baselines that establish the configuration identification of the software at various points in the development cycle.

Example:

Five baselines shall constitute the configuration identification. They are:

Functional baseline
Allocated baseline
Design baseline
Product baseline
Operational baseline

The baselines may be established by labeling the software configuration items and storing them in a central repository or by organizing the configuration items for publication in phase end-documents.

3.2.1 Functional Baseline Configuration Items

This subsection should describe the functional baseline established by the aggregate of configuration items that identify user needs, evaluate the technical and cost feasibility of the systems, and establish the functional requirements of the system.

Example:

The functional baseline shall be established when all the tasks prescribed by the analysis methodology have been completed and the end-items that document the task results have been delivered to the project file and/or have been published in a phase end-document. The document items to be identified shall be categories as follows:

- Initial investigation items include statements of existing problems, projected costs, target schedules, and proposed feasibility study work plans.
- Feasibility study items include statements of the project scope, analyses of problems and constraints, summaries of economic considerations, and recommendations of the project team on future actions to be taken in connection with further development.
- Requirements definition items specify performance, data, environmental, and organizational requirements.

3.2.2 Allocated Baseline Configuration Items

This subsection should describe the allocated baseline established by the aggregate of configuration items that define the distribution of functions to be performed between the hardware and the software components of the system.

Example:

The allocated baseline shall be established when all the tasks prescribed by the external design methodology have been completed and the end-items that document the task results have been delivered to the project file. The document items to be identified shall be categories as follows:

- Software requirements specifications specify how the system will be segmented and how the requirements defined in the functional baseline documents will be allocated to the individual segments.
- Interface control specifications specify the type of interfaces required, the operational implication of each data transfer, the format requirements of interchanged data, and the interface procedures that must be followed.

3.1.3 Design Baseline Configuration Items

This subsection should describe the design baseline that results from the aggregate of configuration items that set forth the design specifications, user procedures and controls and establish plans for implementation and maintenance.

Example:

The design baseline shall be established when all the tasks prescribed by the internal design methodology have been completed and the end-items that document the task results have been delivered to the project file. The document items to be identified shall be categories as follows:

- Input/output specifications detail all of the items that provide input to the system or that are generated as output from the system.
- Data base specifications define the characteristics of the data base files.
- Program specifications provide complete design for each program and subroutine.
- Security and control specifications provide instructions for assembling data, requesting jobs, submitting and receiving information from data processing operations, controlling data base integrity and consistency, restricting data access, controlling errors, and auditing system data.

3.2.4 Product Baseline Configuration Items

This subsection should describe the product baseline that is established when the design specifications have been transformed into executable code and testing has been performed to ensure that the coded programs meet the prescribed requirements.

Example:

The product baseline shall consist of the following document items:

- Program performance specifications prescribe the operational and functional requirements necessary to design, test, and maintain the required programs.

- Program design specifications specify the programming approach for coding the computer programs.
- Program description documents provide complete technical descriptions of all computer subprogram functions, structures, operation environments, operating constraints, and data base organization.
- Program package documents include source/object programs, source/object listings, cross-reference listings, and record layouts.

3.2.5 Operational Baseline Configuration Items

This subsection should describe the operational baseline that is established when the programs have been tested, the conversion process is completed, and a working system is released that conforms to the requirements and specifications.

Example:

The operational baseline shall consist of the following document items:

- Program test documentation includes test plans, test specifications, test procedures, and test reports.
- Conversion documents define file conversion, file creation, and data entry requirements.
- User guides explain the user interactions with the system and summarize the system application and operation functions.
- Training manuals provide instruction for use in classroom presentation.
- Operations documentation defines the control requirements and provides instructions for initiating, running, and terminating the computer system.

Section 4. SOFTWARE CONFIGURATION CONTROL

The policies and procedures used to control established software configurations should be defined in this section.

4.1 Software Configuration Management Documents

This subsection should describe the various documents that are used to control the configuration identification. The document types that should be considered are:

- Policies
- Software change control documents
- Baseline document revision controls
- Standards and guidelines

4.2 Policies

This subsection should review the policies that establish the framework for configuration management, specifically:

- Change initiation policy
- Technical assessment policy
- Approval policy
- Test tracking policy
- Installation policy

4.2.1 Change Initiation Policy

This subsection should review the policy for initiating change and submitting a change request to the change control board for review and approval.

Example:

The following policy statements establish the protocol for requesting changes to configuration items for which identifications have been established:

- The types of changes to be controlled must be identified and documented.
- The activities needed for each category must be defined and documented.
- The review and approval flow of change requests data must be defined and documented.
- The life cycle requirements for responding to change requests must be defined and documented.

4.2.2 Technical Assessment Policy

This subsection should review the policy that addresses the technical impacts on hardware/software, staff training, vendor support, scheduling, testing, backup/recovery, and audit/security.

Example:

The following policy statements establish the protocol for assessing the technical completeness of proposed changes:

- All change requests must be subjected to a technical assessment.
- A plan must be prepared for identifying data, staff, and tools required to perform the technical assessment functions.
- Criteria must be established for evaluating the impact of the proposed changes on the operating environment.
- Criteria must be established for the purpose of evaluating the

adequacy of tests, backup and recovery, and audit and security procedures.

- Individual responsibility for approval or disapproval should be defined.

4.2.3 Business Assessment Policy

This subsection should review the policy that addresses the business impacts of a proposed change.

Example:

The following policy statements establish the protocol for assessing that the proposed changes are compatible with the company's business goals:

- Procedures must be established to facilitate the monitoring of schedules and identifying of timing conflicts which may exist between business and change processing activities.
- Procedures must be established to ensure that all concerned individuals are made aware of the status of changes to configuration items.
- Procedures must be established to support the change coordination functions relative to the business assessment.
- Adequate lead times for conducting the business assessment must be defined.
- Timing conflicts between business requirements and data processing activities should be identified.

4.2.4 Approval Policy

This subsection should review the policy for evaluating the technical and business recommendations and approving or disapproving a change request.

Example:

The following policy statements establish the protocol for approving a change request:

- Procedures must be established for prioritizing and scheduling changes.
- Forms or reports must be designated that reflect the management approval activity.
- Staff assignments and individual responsibilities must be defined for change approval and processing.
- Procedures for monitoring all changes approved for test must be developed.

- Arbitration or escalation processes must be defined.
- Procedures must be established to ensure that only those changes which meet the business and technical assessment criteria are put into effect.

4.2.5 *Test Tracking Policy*

This subsection should review the policy that establishes the framework for monitoring test results.

Example:

The following policy statements establish the protocol for monitoring test results to ensure that changes are tested in a consistent manner:

- Procedures must be established for tracking changes to host computer hardware, remote hardware, host software, communications equipment, and facilities.
- Standards and guidelines must be established for monitoring and controlling test activities.
- Procedures must be established to ensure that all parties who need to know the results of any test activity are adequately informed.
- All backup and recovery procedures must be fully documented and tested.
- The stress levels of each test must be defined and monitored during testing.

4.2.6 *Installation Tracking Policy*

This subsection should review the policy that ensures that the installation of all changes adheres to established standards, change plans, and procedures.

Example:

The following policy statements establish the protocol for tracking the installation progress of all changes to a configuration item:

- A master calendar that provides an overview of the changes to be installed over an extended period of time must be maintained.
- A master calendar that shows the changes to be implemented over the next biweekly period shall be prepared on a weekly basis.
- A mechanism for providing an overview of the planned evolution of the configuration shall be developed for each monthly period.

4.3 Software Change Control Documents

Formal procedures are required to control changes to configuration items. The documents that provide the essential communications are:

- Change classification guidelines
- Change request
- Change action report
- Discrepancy report
- Discrepancy action report
- Status report

4.3.1 Change Classification Guidelines

This subsection should explain how changes are classified and prioritized.

Example:

Change request shall be prioritized as follows:

- Priority Change. This priority shall be designated when immediate action is required, because of potential damage to either the system or its data base.
- Normal Change. This priority is designated when immediate change is not required and normal response times are acceptable.
- Record Change. This priority shall be designated when corrective action has been taken but concurrence on the change is still required.

4.3.2 Change Request

This subsection should provide instructions for preparing a change request (CR) document.

Example:

A change request (CR) document must be prepared for each proposed change to an existing requirement or limitation of the system. The CR must be submitted to the change control board (CCB). The CR may be approved for implementation by the CCB as either a class I or a class II change.

4.3.3 Change Action Report

This subsection should describe the functions of a change action report.

Example:

A change action report (CAR) is the release document for a CR and serves to record and disseminate the action or disposition of the CCB. It may also serve as the release form for any supporting reports or studies required by the CCB to make a proper and informed determination.

4.3.4 Discrepancy Report

This subsection should describe the functions of a discrepancy report.

Example:

A discrepancy report (DR) is prepared to report a discrepancy between the system design documents or between the design documents and a program. It contains information on the discrepancy, criticality, and recommended priority for change, and any proposed solution or corrective action taken. The DR should be submitted to the CCB for approval or disapproval prior to completion of the system installation.

4.3.5 Discrepancy Action Report

This subsection should describe the functions of a discrepancy action report.

Example:

A discrepancy action report (DAR) is the release document to a DR. It serves to record the action or disposition taken on a DR. The DAR contains specific correction instructions for documentation and programs, together with amplifying information such as an analysis of the discrepancy. The DAR will so specify if a DR becomes a CR.

4.3.6 Status Report

This subsection should describe the functions of a status report document.

Example:

A status report document should be prepared on a periodic basis. The CCB shall publish reports of outstanding CRs, CARs, DRs, and DARs and should carry an item for at least one reporting period when action on the item has been completed. Status information must be provided on all approved CRs, CARs, DRs, and DARs until completion of the system installation.

4.4 Baseline Document Revision Control Documents

The documents associated with revision control are:

- Sign-off sheet
- Change control grid

- Document review control form
- Revision control form

4.4.1 Sign-Off Sheet

A sign-off sheet shall be made part of each published work or baseline repository.

Example:

DOCUMENT SIGN-OFF

CATALOG NUMBER:________ **RELEASE DATE:** __________

COSTING SYSTEM

PROGRAM DOCUMENT

Approved By: ________________ **Date:** _______________

Approved By: ________________ **Date:** _______________

Approved By: ________________ **Date:** _______________

4.4.2 Change Control Grid

A change control grid shall be made part of each published work or baseline repository.

Example:

System Name

FEASIBILITY STUDY

REVISION GRID

INSTRUCTIONS:

(1) Place this revision control grid sheet in front of your document.

(2) Cross off each revision number as revisions are received and filed in your document.

1	17	33	49	65	81	97	113	129	145	161
2	18	34	50	66	82	98	114	130	146	162
3	19	35	51	67	83	99	115	131	147	163
4	20	36	52	68	84	100	116	132	148	164
5	21	37	53	69	85	101	117	133	149	165
6	22	38	54	70	86	102	118	134	150	166
7	23	39	55	71	87	103	119	135	151	167
8	24	40	56	72	88	104	120	136	152	168

4.4.3 Document Review Control Form

A document review control form shall be made part of each published work or baseline repository.

Example:

Document Title: ____________ Catalog Number: ____________

☐ Initial Documentation ☐ Change Documentation ☐ Additions

TRANSMITTAL COMMUNICATIONS

Sent To: ____________ Date: ____________

Date Requested For Response: ____________

Action Required:
- ☐ Acknowledgement Of Receipt
- ☐ Review & Response
- ☐ Fill In The Gaps On Page/s ____________
- ☐ Formal Concurrance & Sign-off

ROUTING LIST

Name	Action	By Date

SUMMARY OF RESPONSE

Review Manuscript Received From ____________

- ☐ Corrections/Changes Made As Indicated.
- ☐ Revised Version Prepared & Resubmitted.
- ☐ Revised Version Prepared/Document Finalized.
- ☐ Review Meeting Scheduled ____________

4.4.4 Revision Control Form

A revision control form shall be made part of each published work or baseline repository.

Example:

REVISION CONTROL

Document Title: ____________

Catalog Number: ____________

Check off revision number on Record of Revision sheet in front of manual.

Follow REMOVE and FILE instructions below to update your document.

REMOVE			FILE		
No.	Pages	Dates	No.	Pages	Dates

4.5 Standards and Guidelines

Standards and guidelines should be established for controlling the overall configuration management process.

4.5.1 Interface Control Standards

This subsection should prescribe standards for establishing interface control of all physical and functional interfaces.

Example:

The following statements summarize the standards for establishing interface control of software configuration items:

- Programs entering the acquisition phase shall be broken into two categories: (1) programs requiring a hardware/computer program development cycle and (2) programs requiring a total development cycle.
- The establishment of interface control shall be specified by a request for proposal and the subsequent determination of the following: (1) the designation of a chairperson who shall be responsible for coordinating the interface control functions; (2) the delineation of responsibilities for interface control; and (3) the delineation of responsibilities for status accounting and reporting.
- The relationships, responsibilities, and requirements of the interface control units shall be specified in a statement of work.

4.5.2 Release Requirements Standards

This subsection should prescribe standards for defining the minimum requirements for the release of configuration items.

Example:

The following statements summarize the standards for establishing release requirements:

- Version Construction. The version construction process shall be performed by the CPL. A master copy of each software version shall be maintained by the CPL.
- Integrity Checks. Data checks must be conducted to ensure that the program code and data base files have not changed since the product baseline was established. Regression tests must be performed on each new version before formal verification.
- Traceability. Changes to tapes, decks, etc. must be traceable to the change request that initiated the change. Changes to source programs shall be identifiable in terms of lines, cards, etc. which differ from previous versions. Changes to controlled documentation shall be traceable to the code or instruction change specified in the change initiation function.

Section 5. CONFIGURATION STATUS ACCOUNTING

This section should describe the accounting mechanisms that enable the tracking of and reporting on the status of all configuration items.

5.1 Logs

The following logs should be maintained to list and describe all problem reports, modification records, change notices, and change proposals:

Data base change request log
Design problem report log
Document update transmittal log
Product log
Routine log
Site installation log
Software change proposal log
Software modification report log
Software problem report log
Specification change notice log
Test status log

5.1.1 Data Base Change Request Log

This subsection should describe and illustrate the function of the data base control request log that is used to track all data base change request data.

Example:

The elements of a data base change request log (DBCR) are as follows:

- DBCR no. Identification of the data base change request.
- Requestor.
- Location. Location where the data base resides.
- Modification level. Modification level of the requested data base change.
- Documents affected. List of user and operator manuals that require revision.

5.1.2 Design Problem Report Log

This subsection should describe and illustrate the function of the design problem report log that is used to list all design problem reports submitted for change processing.

Example:

The elements of a Design Problem Report Log are as follows:

- Report no.
- Page/Section. The page and section of the development baseline documents where the problem exists.
- Problem Category.
- Action Required.
- Closure Date. The closure date for each design problem report.

5.1.3 Document Update Transmittal Log

This subsection should describe and illustrate the function of the document update transmittal log that is used to list all design problem reports submitted for change processing.

Example:

The elements of a document update transmittal log are as follows:

- Transmittal form number. The number of the document update transmittal report providing change data.
- Documents to be modified. The identification number and title of the document to be modified.
- Related documents. The name and number of other documents associated with the change.

5.1.4 Product Log

This subsection should describe and illustrate the function of the product log used to list and describe the tapes, disks, decks, disks, and source listings of all released program routines.

Example:

The elements of a product log are as follows:

- Configuration data. The unique configuration item number and the nomenclature of the item type (e.g., binary, source, print, etc.).
- Program routine. The name, ID number, and modification level of the program routine.
- Release data. The date of release and the name of the person authorizing the product release.
- Library catalog no. The library catalog number of the tape, deck, disk, or source listing.

- Distribution. Distribution data showing the number of copies and location of the tapes, decks, source listings, etc.

5.1.5 Routine Log

This subsection should describe and illustrate the function of the routine log used to provide a historical record of each routine's development.

Example:

The elements of a routine log are as follows:

- ID number.
- Routine name.
- Modification number.
- Test cases. List the test cases associated with the software change request
- Tape number.
- Library number.
- Specification number. The number of the product specification which established the configuration item.
- SCP number. The number of the software change proposal (SCP) for which changes to the configuration item have been made.
- Pending SCPs. The identification numbers of software change proposals for which changes are still pending.

5.1.6 Site Installation Log

This subsection should describe and illustrate the function of the site installation log used to identify each site where the software is installed and the software version installed at that site.

Example:

The elements of a site installation log are as follows:

- Title. The title and identification number of the computer program installed.
- Installation accounting. The date the program was installed and the location where the program is installed.
- Verification. The organization authorizing installation.

5.1.7 *Software Change Proposal Log*

This subsection should describe and illustrate the function of the software change proposal log used to track all software change proposals and related software problem reports.

Example:

The elements of a software change proposal log are as follows:

- SCP number. The number of the software change proposal.
- Baseline. The baseline in which the software change proposal was originated.
- Log date.
- Documents affected.
- Program elements affected.

5.1.8 *Software Modification Report Log*

This subsection should describe and illustrate the function of the software modification report log used to track all software modification reports relating to the configuration items.

Example:

The elements of a software modification report log are as follows:

- SMR number. The software modification report (SMR) number.
- Prepared by. The name of the person who prepared the software modification report.
- Problem report number.
- Routine name.
- New modification level number.
- Close date. The date the report was closed.

5.1.9 *Software Problem Report Log*

This subsection should describe and illustrate the function of the software problem report (SPR) log used to maintain surveillance of all submitted problem reports.

Example:

The elements of a software problem report log are as follows:

- SPR number.

- Submitted by:
- Priority.
- Failure analysis number. The number designating the failure analysis category.
- Documents affected. The control numbers of any documentation related to the reported problem.
- Problem closure. The number, date, type of fix, routine modification, and the number of the transmittal form that described the changes to be made to documentation.

5.1.10 Specification Change Notice Log

This subsection should describe and illustrate the function of the specification change notice log used to record all specification change notices.

Example:

The elements of a specification change notice log are as follows:

- Title.
- Revision date.
- Revision number.
- Change classification.
- Affected routines.

5.1.11 Test Status Log

This subsection should describe and illustrate the function of the test status log used to track the test progress of program unit tests, module integration tests, verification tests, and acceptance tests.

Example:

The elements of a Test Status Log are as follows:

- Test name.
- Test function.
- Completion date.
- Data base. The name of the data base involved in testing.
- New version number. The new version number of the tested software.

5.2 Reports

This subsection should provide guidance for the preparation of reports that inform external parties (e.g., project team members, user personnel, etc.) of the status of a configuration item.

Example:

The following reports shall be prepared to inform configuration managers of the status of a configuration item:

- Change request status summary
- Computer program inventory report
- Computer program library (CPL) transmittal summary
- SMR summary
- SPR summary
- Test status summary report

Each of the reports identified in the example above are described and illustrated on the following pages.

5.2.1 Change Request Status Summary

This subsection should describe and illustrate the function of the change request status summary report that is prepared to report the status of all change requests received and logged during a given period.

Example:

The elements of a change request status summary report are as follows:

- Report number.
- Date.
- Change request number. The number of each change request logged.
- Change classification. The classification identification of each change request logged.
- Action. The actions taken and/or pending on each change request that was logged.

5.2.2 Computer Program Inventory Report

This subsection should describe and illustrate the function of the computer program inventory report that is prepared to provide visibility of the configuration items in the computer program library.

Example:

The elements of a computer program inventory report are as follows:

- Report number.
- Date.
- Application programs. A list of all application programs showing release number and version ID.
- Test software. A list of all test software showing release number and version ID.
- Documentation. A list of documentation showing release number and version ID.
- Data base items. A list of data base items showing release number and version ID.
- Test data files. A list of all test data on computer-sensible media showing release number and version ID.

5.2.3 Computer Program Library Transmittal Summary

This subsection should describe and illustrate the function of the computer program library transmittal summary that is prepared to report on the transmittal forms logged and the subsequent actions taken during the reporting period.

Example:

The elements of a computer program library transmittal summary are as follows:

- Report number.
- Date.
- SCI number. The identification number of the program, document, or test case being transmitted to the CPL.
- Transmittal form number.
- Transmittal date.
- CPL data. The index numbers of the base version and new version and the release date.
- Related documents. The number of any related software problem reports or software modification reports.

5.2.4 Software Modification Report Summary

This subsection should describe and illustrate the function of the software modification report summary that is prepared to report on the actions taken on SMRs received during a specified period.

Example:

The elements of a software modification report summary are as follows:

- Report number.
- Date.
- SCI number. The identification number of the program, document, or test case being transmitted to the CPL.
- SMR number.
- SMR date. The date of each applicable SMR report.
- Action. The actions taken and or pending, showing the date logged, date implemented, and the associated discrepancy or change request.

5.2.5 Software Problem Report Summary

This subsection should describe and illustrate the function of the software problem report summary that is prepared to report on the status reports received and the actions taken on the reported problems during a specified period.

Example:

The elements of a software problem report summary are as follows:

- SCI number. The identification number of the software configuration item (SCI).
- SPR number.
- SPR date.
- Date logged.
- Date implemented.
- DR/DAR number.

5.2.6 Test Status Summary Report

This subsection should describe and illustrate the function of the test status summary report that is prepared to summarize the status of all program tests.

Example:

The elements of a test status summary report are as follows:

- Report number.
- Date.

- Tests run.
- Test results.
- Tests pending.
- Scheduled test date. The schedule status of the various tests.

5.3 Version Description Documents

This subsection should describe and illustrate the sectional breakdown of the version description document (VDD) that should accompany the release of each version of a program configuration item.

Example:

The sectional elements of a version description document are as follows:

- Version identification. This subsection of the VDD shall identify the software configuration item by its unique number, briefly describe the item, and indicate its delivery medium.
- Version application. This subsection of the VDD shall explain the application of the version and identify superseded versions and other versions still in use.
- Differences between versions. This subsection of the VDD shall explain the functional differences of the various versions.
- Software capabilities and limitations. This subsection of the VDD shall summarize the limitations on software operations imposed by the changes and the capabilities of the version documented.
- Adaptation information. This subsection of the VDD shall record the changes required to adapt the equipment, operations, or system usage to the new version.
- Installation instructions. This subsection of the VDD shall outline the procedures for installing the software version in the operational environment.

Section 6. SOFTWARE CONFIGURATION AUDITING

The verification and validation process shall involve three separate audit functions:

- Functional configuration audit (FCA)
- Physical configuration audit (PCA)
- Formal qualification review (FQR)

6.1 Functional Configuration Audit

The function of the FCA is to verify that all unit tests specified in the test plan have been completed and that the software configuration item, based on test results, meets the functional and allocated requirements. The primary documents associated with the conduct of the FCA are checklists, questionnaires, verification forms, and audit records. These working papers provide a means for recording and evaluating the evidence collected during the FCA. The functions of each type of working paper are described below and on the following pages.

6.1.1 FCA Checklists

Checklists of all the functional and allocated performance requirements should be prepared prior to initiating the FCA. These checklists are used in analyzing test reports to determine if the configuration item established at the product baseline meets the requirements that were defined at the functional and allocated baselines.

Example:

FUNCTIONAL REQUIREMENTS CHECKLIST

SPEC NO.	SPECIFICATION	AUDITING FACTORS		
		Performance Requirements	Environments Requirements	Data Requirements
2.1	ACCURACY AND VALIDITY	X		
2.2	TIMING	X		
2.3.1	Backup	X		
2.3.2	Fallback	X		
2.3.3	Restart	X		
3.1	EQUIPMENT ENVIRONMENT		X	
3.1.1	Processors		X	
3.1.2	Storage Media		X	
3.1.3	Input Device(s)		X	
3.1.4	Communications			
3.2	SUPPORT SOFTWARE EQUIPMENT		X	
3.2.1	Support Software		X	
3.2.2	Input & Equipment Siumulators		X	
3.2.3	Test Software		X	
3.2.4	Utilities		X	
3.2.5	Operating System		X	
3.2.6	Data Management Systems		X	
3.3	INTERFACES		X	
3.4	SECURITY AND PRIVACY		X	
3.5	CONTROL REQUIREMENTS			

6.1.2 Questionnaires

To facilitate the interview process, the auditor shall prepare questionnaires that list the questions to be asked in gathering information about performance problems and requirements.

Example:

FCA AUDIT QUESTIONNAIRE			
QUESTION NO.	**REFERENCE SPEC.**	**QUESTION**	**INTERVIEWEE**
1	FB 2.1	Are there accuracy and validity requirements beyond those specified in section 2.1 of the functional baseline?	
2	FB 2.2	Are there timing requirements agreed upon but undocumented in the functional baseline document?	
3	FB 2.3	Are there failure requirements agreed upon, but undocumented in the functional baseline document?	
4	FB 3	Does the system installed meet the requirements as specified?	
5	FB 3.1	Do the equipment specifications in the functional baseline reflect all of the actual requirements?	
6	FB 3.2	Were the interface requirements for gathering data completely satisfied?	

6.1.3 Worksheets

FCA worksheets shall made a part of the audit repository.

Example:

The auditor's worksheets shall be retained in the FCA repository. The elements of a typical worksheet are as follows:

- Name of the person interviewed.
- Date and location of interview.
- Question number.
- Interviewee's response. A summary response of the person interviewed.
- References/attachments. Description of any documentation or references provided by interviewee.

6.1.4 Interview Summary

The auditor will prepare an interview summary that shall be maintained as permanent working papers.

Example:

The interview summary prepared by the auditor should summarize the information gathered from the interviews. The elements of a typical interview summary are:

- Question number. The number of the question on the questionnaire.
- Respondent's initials. The respondent's identification/initials.
- Response summary. A summary of the information gathered during the interview.

6.1.5 FCA Verification Form

This subsection should describe and illustrate the sectional breakdown of the FCA verification form that the auditor prepares to verify that test results for a configuration item coincide with the functional and allocated requirement.

Example:

The sectional elements of the FCA verification form shall be as follows:

- Accuracy and validity. This subsection of the FCA verification form shall verify the accuracy and validity of the current status of a configuration item.
- Data integrity. This subsection of the FCA verification form shall summarize the data integrity audit factors.
- Performance verification form. This subsection of the FCA verification form shall summarize the performance audit factors.

6.2 Physical Configuration Audit

The functions of the PCA are to verify the adequacy and accuracy of the documentation. To accomplish this objective, the following checklists should be prepared to guide the audit process:

- Design documentation checklist
- Test documentation checklist
- Version description documentation checklist
- Change control documentation checklist

6.2.1 Design Documentation Checklist

To verify the adequacy, accuracy, and completeness of the design documentation, a checklist should be prepared to facilitate the physical audit.

Example:

The elements of a design documentation checklist are as follows:

- General. A checklist of project references and indexes (e.g., index of programs, index of files, etc.).
- Inputs and outputs. A checklist of input document formats, input

screen formats, output document formats, and output screen formats.

- Data base specifications. A checklist of labeling/tagging conventions, data base organization factors, special instructions, file layouts, table layouts, and record layouts.
- Program specifications. A checklist of interfaces, storage requirements, and program design specifications.
- Controls and security. A checklist of I/O controls, user controls, data base/file controls, access controls, error controls, and audit trails.
- Backup/recovery. A checklist of backup procedures, file retention procedures, and restart procedures.

6.2.2 Test Documentation Checklist

To verify the adequacy, accuracy, and completeness of the documentation that defines the test specifications and test evaluation procedures, a checklist should be prepared to facilitate the physical audit.

Example:

The elements of a test documentation checklist are as follows:

- Computer program test plan. A checklist of training requirements, test management requirements, personnel requirements, hardware requirements, and supporting software requirements.
- Computer program test specifications. A checklist of testing requirements, test management requirements, personnel requirements, hardware requirements, and supporting software requirements.
- Computer program test procedures. A checklist of testing requirements, test management requirements, personnel requirements, hardware requirements, and supporting software requirements.
- Computer program test report. A checklist of test results, evaluation criteria, test evaluation documents, and recommendations.

6.2.3 Version Description Documentation Checklist

To verify the adequacy, accuracy, and completeness of the documentation that identifies the current version and describes the version capabilities, a checklist should be prepared to facilitate the physical audit.

Example:

A checklist shall be prepared to verify the adequacy and completeness of the documentation related to each version of a software configuration item. The elements of a version description documentation Checklist are as follows:

- Change summary
- Limitations
- Adaptation information
- Interface compatibility
- Changes
- Installation instructions

6.2.4 Change Control Documentation Checklist

To verify the adequacy, accuracy, and completeness of the logs and status reports that are used to monitor changes to a configuration item, a checklist should be prepared to facilitate the physical audit.

Example:

A checklist shall be prepared to verify the adequacy and completeness of the documentation related to each software configuration item. The elements of a change control documentation checklist are as follows:

- Change classification index. Indicate documentation status (i.e., complete, current, accurate).
- Change requests. Indicate documentation status (i.e., complete, current, accurate).
- Change action report. Indicate documentation status (i.e., complete, current, accurate).
- Discrepancy report. Indicate documentation status (i.e., complete, current, accurate).
- Discrepancy action report. Indicate documentation status (i.e., complete, current, accurate).
- Status report. Indicate documentation status (i.e., complete, current, accurate).

6.3 Formal Qualification Review

The purpose of the formal qualification review is to establish that the software configuration item performs in its operating environment. A configuration audit record should be prepared to document the FQR process.

Example:

The elements of a configuration audit record are as follows:

- SCI number.
- SCI name.
- FCA start/complete dates.
- PCA start/complete dates.
- FQR start/complete dates.

2.3 Summary

A software configuration management plan is a document that describes the requirements for configuration identification, control, accounting, and auditing. It also defines the procedures for implementing the configuration management of baseline identifications and identifies the persons and organizations who will be responsible for carrying out the procedures.

In preparing a software configuration management plan, certain parameters have to be defined. Specifically, criteria should be established for each of the following elements of a configuration management plan.

General. In a general context, the plan should reflect the documentation identified by the systems development methodology, agree with the phased development of the methodology, establish requirements for quality assurance, and identify the support needed to effectively manage a software configuration.

Organization. The organizational structure should be adequately defined. An organization chart should also be included.

Identification. The software configuration management plan should identify the documentation that will be controlled, the numbering and marking systems, and the SCIs that comprise each baseline. It should explain the logic for identifying SCIs and specify those standards that must be used in the identification process.

Control. The software configuration management plan should define the change classification scheme and specify those milestones at which changes can be introduced. Procedures for change processing, including forms and diagrams, should be detailed and illustrated.

Status Accounting. The software configuration management plan should specify the data required for configuration status accounting and the methods to be used. The forms, formats, and procedures for preparing status reports should be clearly delineated. Examples of the reports should also be included.

Audit. The software configuration management plan should indicate the types of audits to be conducted and who will conduct the audits. Step-by-step procedures for conducting audits should be included.

Interface Control. The software configuration plan should identify procedures to be used to control all hardware and software interfaces. It should identify the responsibilities and authorities of those responsible for interface control. The forms and reports to be used in controlling interfaces should be identified and illustrated.

Chapter

3

Software Configuration Identification

The basis of software configuration management is the identification of the items that comprise the software product at each point of its development. The software configuration items (SCIs) evolve during the development cycle. However, the ability to establish a known baseline allows for controlled changes without risking the overall development.

A baseline may be established in two ways: by labeling the SCIs and storing them in a project file or by organizing the SCIs for publication in a phase end-document. In either case, identification of SCIs is essential to achieve traceability through all phases of development.

SCIs may exist in a variety of forms, and each form may exist on a variety of media. SCIs include computer programs that satisfy operational, support, utility, training, maintenance, and testing requirements; documentation that records the results of the analysis, design, programming, and testing phases of systems development; computer listings of program code, data base definitions, or data base values; hardware specifications for processors, direct access storage devices (DASD), and peripherals; software specifications for communications and data base management; hardware and software change releases; version description documents that identify the current version and describe the version capabilities; implementation documentation, including user and operations guides and training manuals; and vendor documents that reference the purchased hardware and software used within the operating environment.

In addition to identifying each SCI in the software development cycle, the collection of SCIs into baselines associated with the phases or stages of the development life cycle is essential for the control of changes and for ensuring completion of each task in the development effort. Each baseline constitutes a measurable milestone which can be recreated from the SCI identification.

Five baselines for identification are recommended: *functional baseline, allocated baseline, design baseline, product baseline,* and *operational baseline*. The baseline management concept is used both for configuration control established at a point in the system life cycle at the option of the developer and for configuration control that is compliant with preestablished procedures. The configuration control board (CCB) bears the primary responsibility for baseline management relative to the systematic evaluation, coordination, and disposition of all changes to the established baselines.

The tasks associated with the identification of the software configuration are shown in Figure 3-1 and detailed in this chapter.

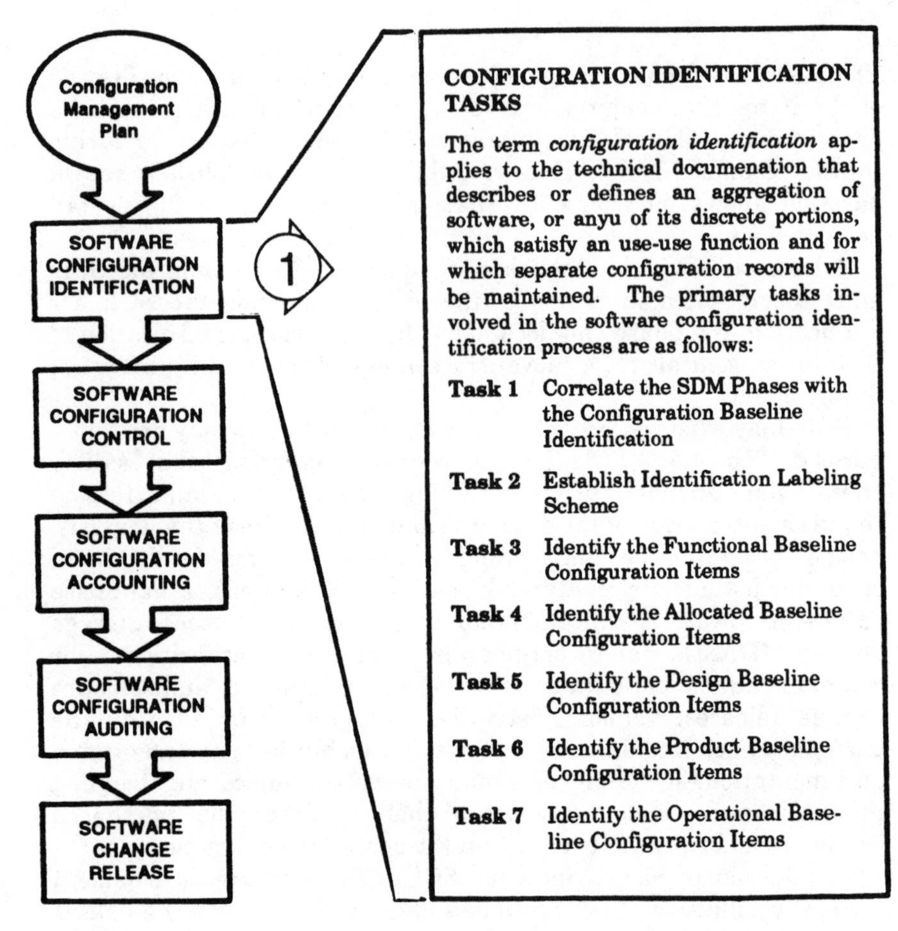

Figure 3-1. Software Configuration Identification Tasks

3.1 Task 1: Correlate the SDM Phases with the Configuration Baseline Identification

The first task in establishing a configuration identification is to define the milestones in the development cycle where the identification is to occur. The development of a software product proceeds through several stages or phases, commonly referred to as the *system life cycle*. Each phase of development marks a measurable progress point in the development cycle. To effectively manage the software development process, the results of the tasks performed during each phase of development must be properly identified. The documented results are called *software configuration items* (SCIs). The aggregate of SCIs for a particular stage of development provides a baseline that establishes the configuration identification of the software at that point in the development cycle. Figure 3-2 depicts the phases of the system life cycle, showing the baseline that establishes the configuration identification at each stage.

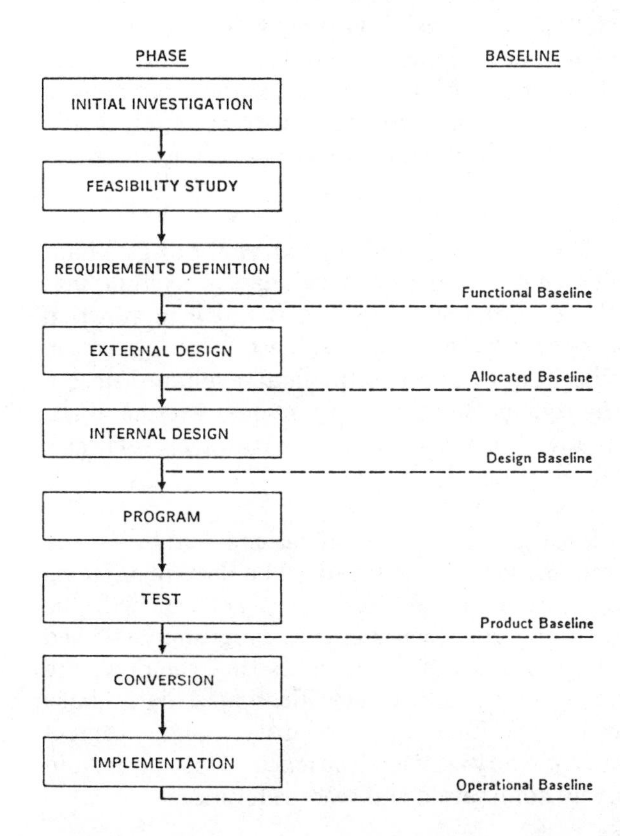

Figure 3-2. Baseline Correlation of Life-Cycle Stages

3.1.1 Baseline Management

One of the more important aspects of configuration management is the concept of baseline management. Baseline management is formally required at the beginning of a software development effort and may be redefined at any point in the development process where it may be necessary to define a formal departure point for control of future changes in performance and design.

In a conventional product development environment there are usually only three baselines: functional, allocated, and product. In a data processing environment, however, five baselines are recommended that correlate with the functional objectives of a typical systems development methodology.

The following baselines form the basic requirements for software configuration control.

Functional Baseline. The easiest way to identify the documentation that establishes the functional baseline for configuration management is to follow the task documentation orientation prescribed by the analysis methodology. The document items that comprise the baseline include those documents that define the problem and need, project costs and target schedules, analyze the present and proposed systems, and define performance, environment, and data requirements.

Allocated Baseline. The deliverables of the external design phase of systems development that focuses on dividing the system into subsystems establish the allocated baseline for software configuration management. The baseline documentation subject to configuration change control includes those documents that evaluate design alternatives; define the system/subsystem functions, system data, and processing logic; and specify technical, hardware, software, operating, security, and interface requirements.

Design Baseline. Internal design specifications establish the design baseline for configuration management. The document items produced during this phase detail how the system will be implemented and provide the specifications that programmers need to code the modules. The specification documents that comprise the design baseline include input/output specifications, data base specifications; program specifications, security and control specifications, backup/recovery specifications; testing and implementation plans, and summaries and cross-references.

Product Baseline. Program and test documentation establishes the product baseline for configuration management. The documentation includes program performance and design specifications; program description documents; program package documents; test plans, test specifications, test procedures, and test reports.

Operational Baseline. The documentation for systems implementation establishes the operational baseline for configuration management. In a well-defined software development environment, however, the preparation of implementation documents is essentially an iterative process that synthesizes and reorganizes document items that were produced during the analysis and design phases for presentation to a user audience. Implementation documentation may be grouped and presented in the following document types that are subject to configuration control: conversion documents, user guides, operations guides, and training manuals.

Once defined, changes in the baseline SCIs must be formally approved and documented.

3.1.2 Configuration Items

A baseline identification comprises the aggregate of the software items that were delivered to the project file during the phase(s) of development that correlate with an established baseline. The presentation contained here represents baselines that correlate with a systems development methodology that divides the development process into nine phases:

- Initial investigation
- Feasibility study
- Requirements definition
- External design
- Internal design
- Programming
- Test
- Conversion
- Implementation

Not all these phases, of course, may characterize every software development project. Therefore, in consultation with the project managers, the configuration manager should, at the beginning of each project, determine precisely the phases of the system life cycle and the document types to be produced. The baselines should then be mapped to correlate with those development phases. In a small systems environment, it is frequently necessary to combine certain of the development phases. For example, the initial investigation, feasibility study, and requirements definition phases may be combined into one phase called *assessment analysis*.

3.2 Task 2: Establish Identification Labeling Scheme

Once the baselines have been established in relation to the development phases, a method for uniquely identifying each SCI must be established. As noted earlier, the SCIs that establish the various baselines may be identified as components of a project file or as sections, subsections, or paragraphs of a phase end-document. The repository of SCIs in either form requires a labeling scheme that enables each SCI to be readily identified. The labeling elements to be considered are as follows:

1st labeling element = project identification

2d labeling element = baseline identification

3d labeling element = phase identification

4th labeling element = subphase identification

5th labeling element = 1st level baseline SCIs

6th labeling element = 2nd level baseline SCIs

7th labeling element = 3rd level baseline SCIs

8th labeling element = 4th level baseline SCIs

SCIs may exist in a multiplicity of media. The labeling scheme may be expanded to include the media identification. The primary media forms in which SCIs are stored are as follows:

- Documents
- Physical items (e.g., tapes, disks, etc.)
- Machine-readable items (program code, JCL, etc.)

The data dictionary may be used to catalog SCIs and to cross-reference the media forms in which the SCIs exist. Additionally, library control software is available for managing the configuration identifications of program libraries on the computer. These packages can facilitate the management of the complete software identification. The multiplicity of media, however, generally requires a manual control in addition to the automated tools.

Figure 3-3 further illustrates the hierarchy of the labeling scheme.

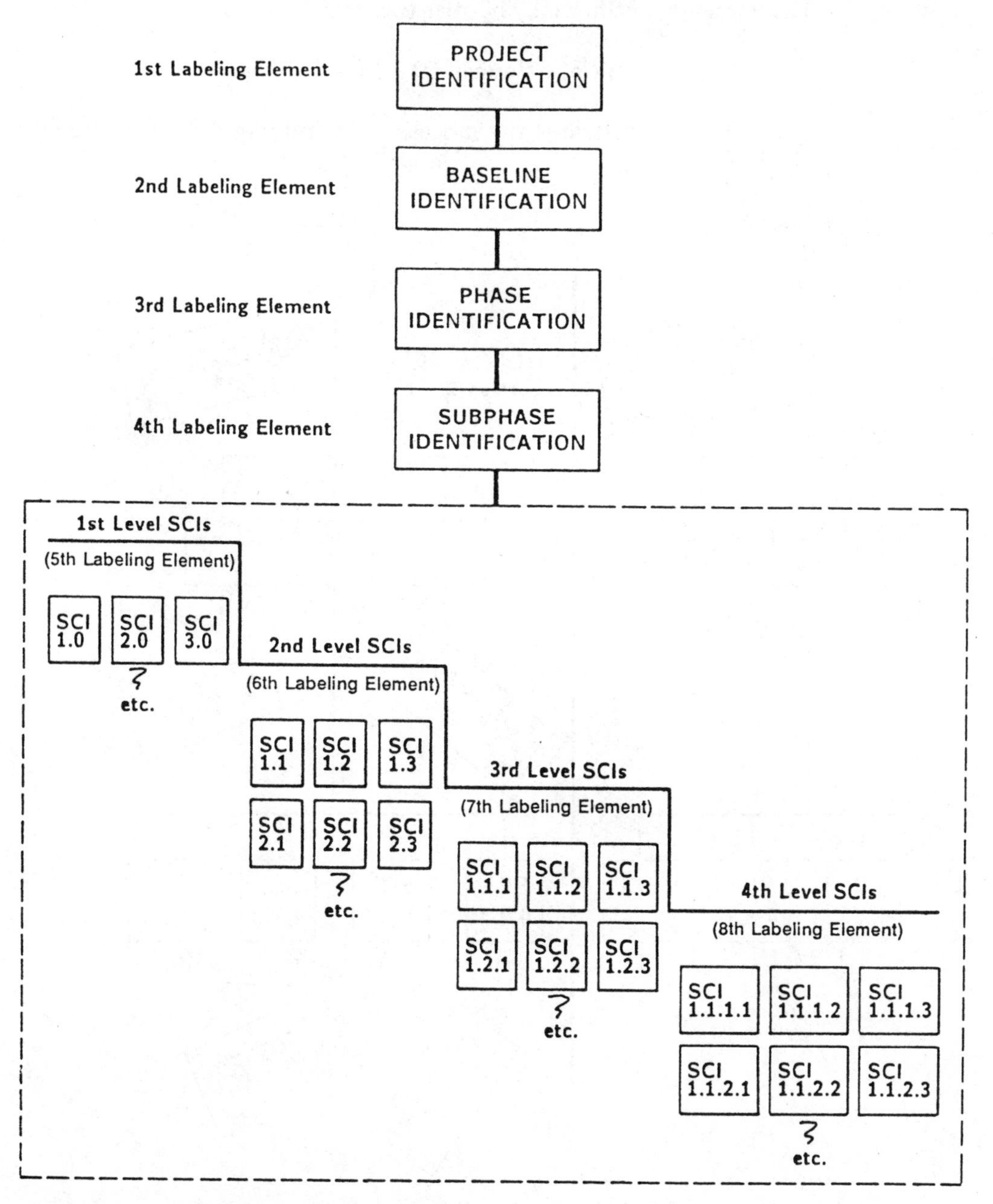

Figure 3-3. Hierarchy of an SCI Labeling Scheme

In addition to identifying the SCIs maintained in a project file or contained in a baseline document, a labeling scheme is needed to distinguish between versions of the same SCI. The labeling scheme should be devised to facilitate traceability of all changes to an SCI. The version identifier may be structured as follows:

Release No. + Version ID + Date of Release

Figure 3-4 illustrates the process of identifying different versions of an SCI.

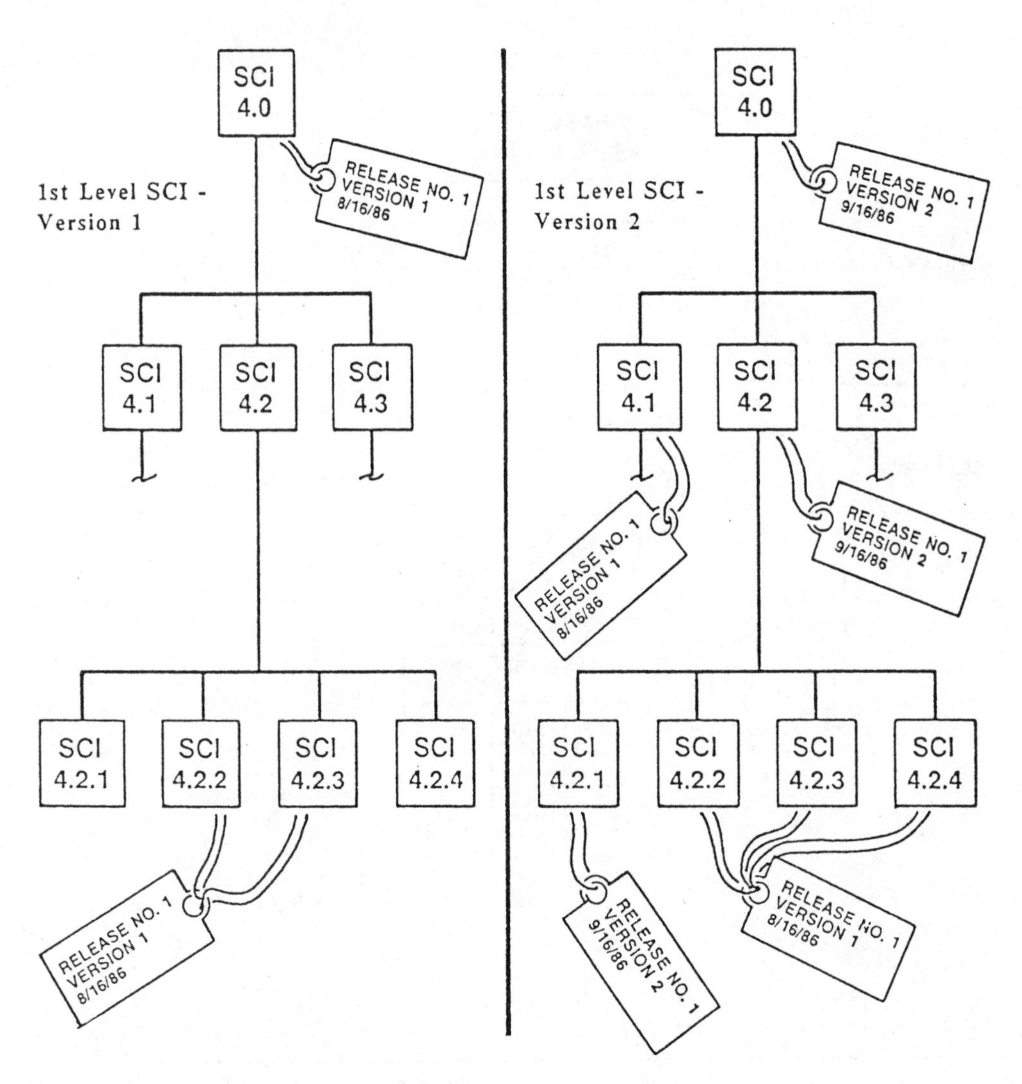

Figure 3-4. SCI Version Identification

3.3 Task 3: Identify the Functional Baseline Configuration Items

The functional baseline is established when SCIs have been identified that define user needs, evaluate the technical and cost feasibility of the proposed system, and establish the functional requirements. The labeling scheme for identifying functional baseline SCIs is outlined in Table 3-1.

Table 3-1. Functional Baseline SCI Labeling Scheme

Software Configuration Item	SCI Level	Label
FUNCTIONAL BASELINE REPOSITORY	**BASELINE**	**FB**
Initial Investigation Phase End-Document/Repository	**Phase**	**II**
Management Summary	*II 1st level*	*1.0*
Problem and Need Statement	II 2d level	1.1
Preliminary Costs Analysis	II 2d level	1.2
Target Schedule	II 2d level	1.3
Feasibility Study Work Plan	*II 1st level*	*2.0*
Present System Review	II 2d level	2.1
Proposed System Requirements	II 2d level	2.2
Applications Package Review	II 2d level	2.3
Economic Evaluation	II 2d level	2.4
Feasibility Study Phase End-Document/Repository	**Phase**	**FS**
Present System Review	*FS 1st level*	*1.0*
Present System Schematic	FS 2d level	1.1
Organizational/Personnel Responsibilities	FS 2d level	1.2
Equipment Requirements	FS 2d level	1.3
System Requirements	FS 2d level	1.4
List of Programs	FS 2d level	1.5
List of Inputs	FS 2d level	1.6
List of Outputs	FS 2d level	1.7
Data Base/File Summary	FS 2d level	1.8
Summary of Controls	FS 2d level	1.9
Documentation Index	FS 2d level	1.10
Cost Statement	FS 2d level	1.11

Table 3-1. Functional Baseline SCI Labeling Scheme (*Continued*)

Software Configuration Item	SCI Level	Label
FUNCTIONAL BASELINE REPOSITORY	**BASELINE**	**FB**
Proposed System Requirements	*FS 1st level*	*2.0*
Proposed System Schematic	FS 2d level	2.1
Statement of Objectives	FS 2d level	2.2
Summary of Improvements	FS 2d level	2.3
New Capabilities	FS 3d level	2.3.1
Upgrading Existing Capabilities	FS 3d level	2.3.2
Summary of Impacts	FS 2d level	2.4
Equipment Impacts	FS 3d level	2.4.1
Software Impacts	FS 3d level	2.4.2
Organizational Impacts	FS 3d level	2.4.3
Operational Impacts	FS 3d level	2.4.4
Development Impacts	FS 3d level	2.4.5
Assumptions and Constraints	FS 2d level	2.5
Applications Package Review	*FS 1st level*	*3.0*
List of Available Packages	FS 2d level	3.1
Economic Evaluation	*FS 1st level*	*4.0*
Benefit Statement	FS 2d level	4.1
Cost Report	FS 2d level	4.2
Requirements Definition Phase End-Document/Repository	**Phase**	**RD**
General Statements	*RD 1st level*	*1.0*
Statement of Baseline Purpose	RD 2d level	1.1
Project References	RD 2d level	1.2
Terms and Abbreviations	RD 2d level	1.3
Security and Privacy	RD 2d level	1.4
Performance Requirements	*RD 1st level*	*2.0*
Accuracy and Validity Requirements	RD 2d level	2.1
Timing Requirements	RD 2d level	2.2
Failure Contingencies	RD 2d level	2.3
Backup Contingencies	RD 3d level	2.3.1
Fall-back Contingencies	RD 3d level	2.3.2
Restart Contingencies	RD 3d level	2.3.2

Table 3-1. Functional Baseline SCI Labeling Scheme (*Continued*)

Software Configuration Item	SCI Level	Label
FUNCTIONAL BASELINE REPOSITORY	**BASELINE**	**FB**
Environment Requirements	*RD 1st level*	*3.0*
Equipment Requirements	RD 2d level	3.1
Support Software Requirements	RD 2d level	3.2
Interface	RD 2d level	3.3
Security and Privacy	RD 2d level	3.4
Control Requirements	RD 2d level	3.5
Data Requirements	*RD 1st level*	*4.0*
Data Descriptions	RD 2d level	4.1
Static System Data	RD 3d level	4.1.1
Dynamic Input Data	RD 3d level	4.1.2
Dynamic Output Data	RD 3d level	4.1.3
System Data Constraints	RD 3d level	4.1.4
Data Collection Requirements	RD 2d level	4.2
Input Formats	RD 2d level	4.3
Output Formats	RD 2d level	4.4
Data Base Impacts	RD 2d level	4.5
Package Evaluation	*RD 1st level*	*5.0*
Evaluation Criteria	RD 2d level	5.1

As shown in Figure 3-1, the functional baseline repository consists of three categories of SCIs: initial investigation, feasibility study, and requirements definition.

The *initial investigation* SCIs include statements of existing problems, projected costs, target schedules, and feasibility study workplans.

Feasibility study SCIs compare the present system to the proposed system and identify costs and consequences. They describe how the proposed system will function and how it will solve the problems that were defined during the initial investigation.

Requirements definition SCIs identify the types and frequency of inputs and outputs, describe the required data bases or files, establish system controls, and explain the required interfaces.

These three sets of SCIs jointly form the functional baseline for software configuration management.

In summary, the physical content of the functional baseline

repository provides the economic, operational, and technical information that management needs to make decisions on the initial feasibility of a project request. It also establishes the functional requirements of the proposed system. The configuration items that establish this baseline will be expanded upon in subsequent phases and contribute to the establishment of the next baseline. It is important, therefore, that the items be readily available through either the project file or the data dictionary to facilitate the next steps of development and to evaluate suggested changes to the functional requirements of the software system.

Figure 3-5 illustrates the project file and phase end-document orientation related to the organization of functional baseline SCIs

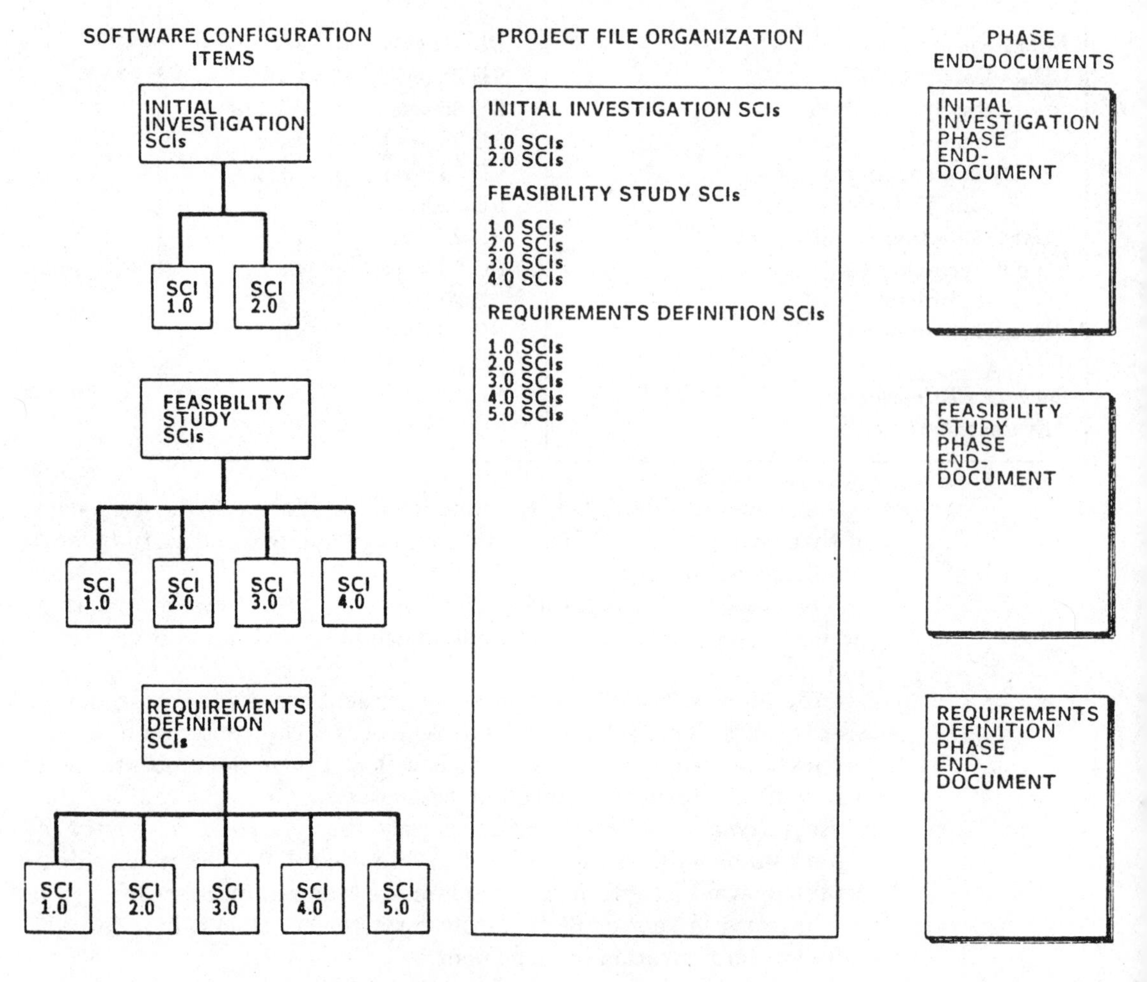

Figure 3-5. Project File/ Phase End-Document Orientation of Functional Baseline

As previously noted, the life-cycle phases of the software development methodology define the baselines for configuration management. Each phase specified by the methodology is further broken down into a series of tasks and task steps. The results of these tasks and task steps are recorded at the completion of each task. When the task results have been fully documented, the document items are delivered to a project file and placed under configuration control. The process as it relates to the functional baseline for configuration management is shown in Figure 3-6.

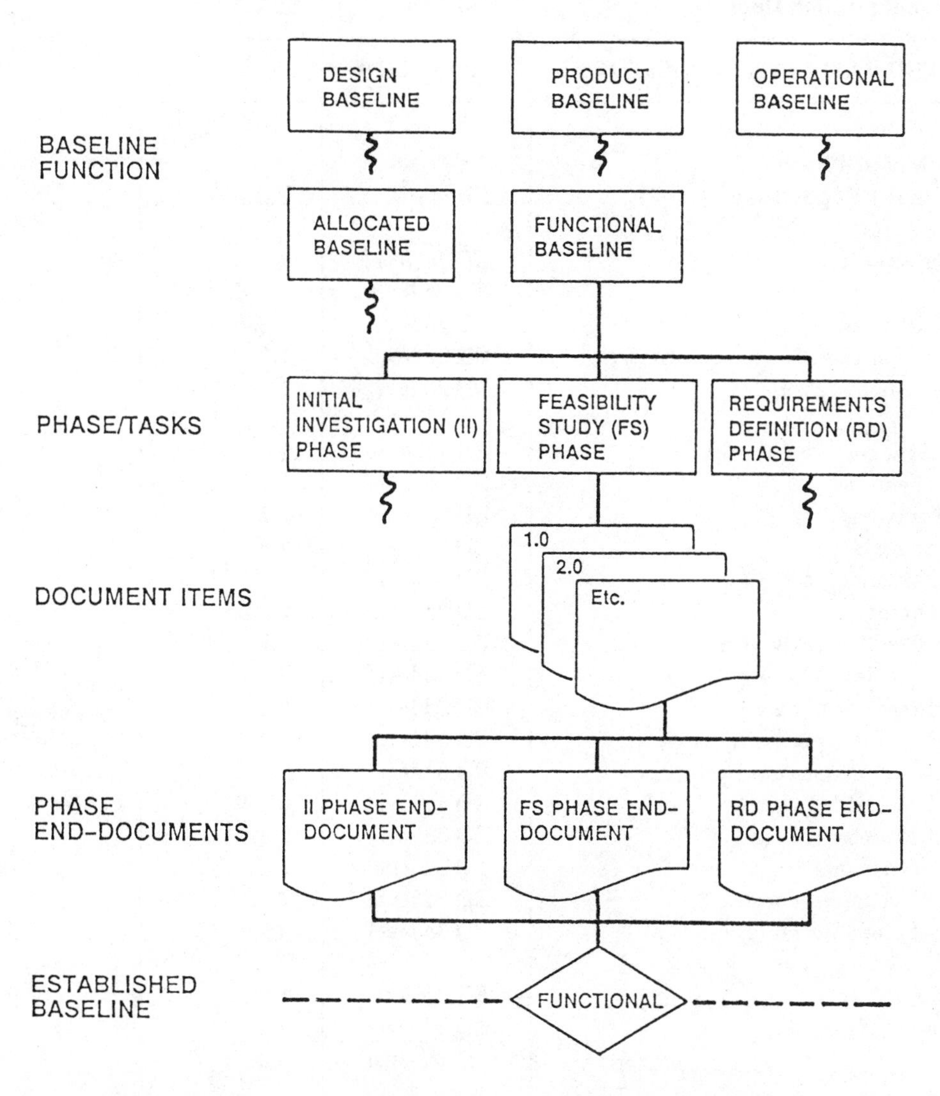

Figure 3-6. End-Document Orientation of the Analysis Process

3.4 Task 4: Identify the Allocated Baseline Configuration Items

The allocated baseline is established when SCIs have been identified that define the specific hardware and software functions to be performed. The labeling scheme for identifying allocated baseline SCIs is outlined in Table 3-2.

Table 3-2. Allocated Baseline SCI Labeling Scheme

Software Configuration Item	SCI Level	Label
ALLOCATED BASELINE REPOSITORY	**BASELINE**	**FB**
External Design Phase End-Document/Repository	**Phase**	**ED**
General Statements	*ED 1st level*	*1.0*
Statement of Purpose	ED 2d level	1.1
Project References	ED 2d level	1.2
Application Package/Chosen Alternative	ED 2d level	1.3
Terms and Abbreviations	ED 2d level	1.4
System / Subsystem Specifications	*ED 1st level*	*2.0*
System Schematic	ED 2d level	2.1
System Functions	ED 2d level	2.2
System Input Data	ED 2d level	2.3
Source Documents	ED 3d level	2.3.1
File Content	ED 3d level	2.3.2
Inputs from Other Systems	ED 3d level	2.3.3
Processing Logic	ED 2d level	2.4
Input Processing Logic	ED 3d level	2.4.1
Data Base/File Processing Logic	ED 3d level	2.4.2
History File Processing Logic	ED 3d level	2.4.3
Table Processing Logic	ED 3d level	2.4.4
Output Processing Logic	ED 3d level	2.4.5
Output Descriptions	ED 2d level	2.5
Output Document Formats	ED 3d level	2.5.1
Output Screen Formats	ED 3d level	2.5.2
Security and Controls	*ED 1st level*	*3.0*
Security and Privacy	ED 2d level	3.1
Controls	ED 2d level	3.2

Table 3-2. Allocated Baseline SCI Labeling Scheme *(Continued)*

Software Configuration Item	SCI Level	Label
ALLOCATED BASELINE REPOSITORY	**BASELINE**	**FB**
Technical Environment	*ED 1st level*	*4.0*
Hardware Considerations	ED 2d level	4.1
Software Considerations	ED 2d level	4.2
Performance Criteria	ED 2d level	4.3
Acceptance Response Time	ED 3d level	4.3.1
System-Up Time Window	ED 3d level	4.3.2
Backup Considerations	ED 2d level	4.4
Interfacing Requirements	*ED 1st level*	*5.0*
Hardware Interfaces	ED 2d level	5.1
Software Interfaces	ED 2d level	5.2

The project file and phase end-document orientation of the allocated baseline SCIs is illustrated in Figure 3-7.

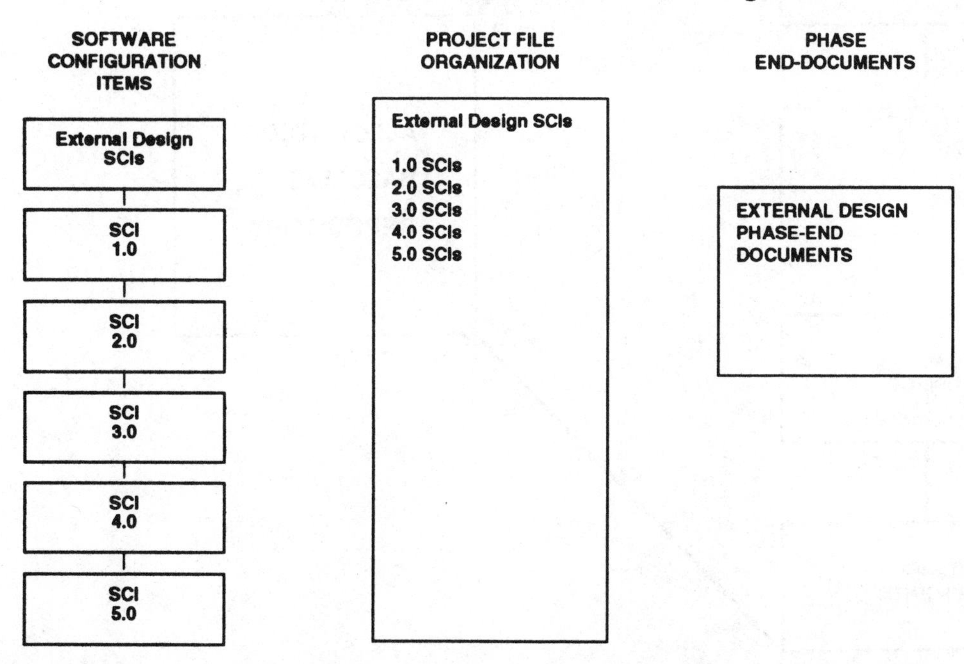

Figure 3-7. Project File/Phase End-Document Orientation of Allocated Baseline

The document items that translate the functional requirements into performance-oriented development specifications and allocate the functional design description to specific subsystems establish the allocated baseline. The document items may be categorized as follows: specifications that define how the system will be segmented and how the requirements defined in the functional baseline documents will be allocated to the individual segments and interface control specifications that establish the performance requirements of both hardware and software interfaces required by the system. Figure 3-8 illustrates the development of the allocated baseline repository.

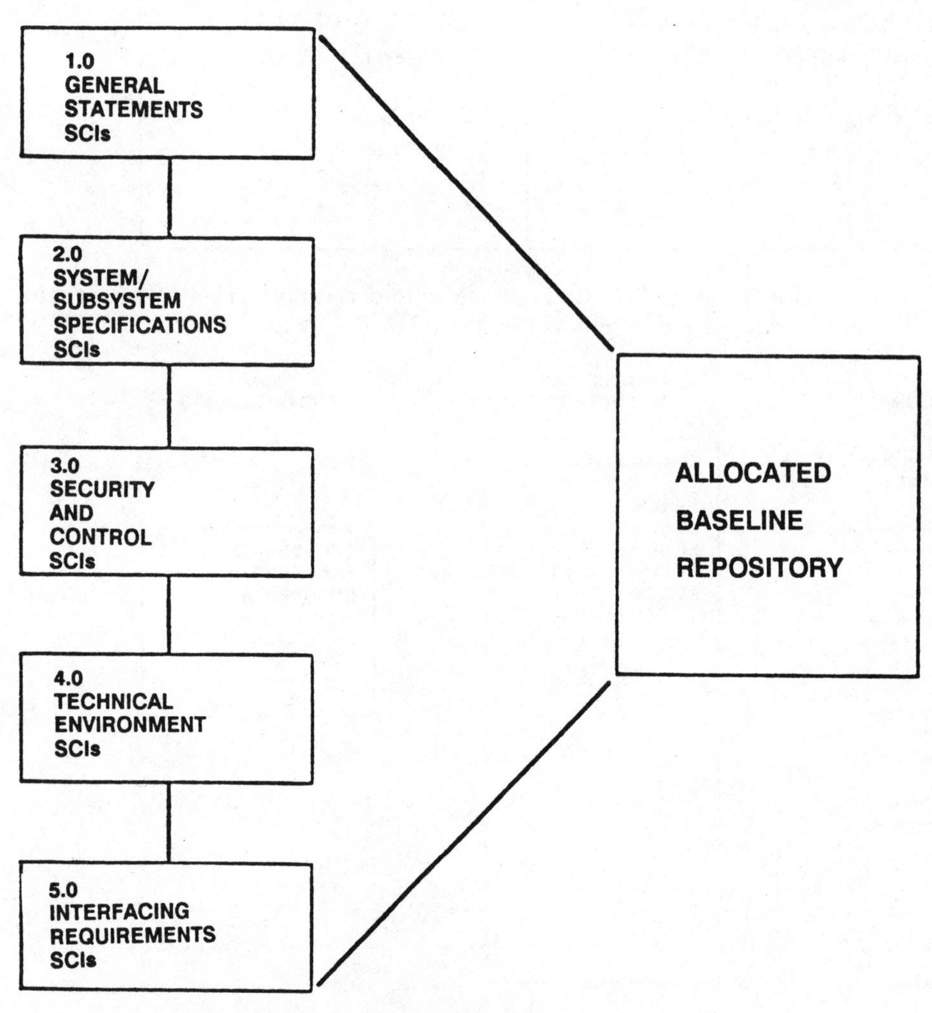

Figure 3-8. Allocated Baseline Repository

3.5 Task 5: Identify the Design Baseline Configuration Items

The design baseline results from the aggregate of SCIs that set forth the design specifications, define the user procedures and controls, and establish plans for implementation and maintenance. The labeling scheme for identifying design baseline SCIs is outlined in Table 3-3.

Table 3-3. Design Baseline SCI Labeling Scheme

Software Configuration Item	SCI Level	Label
DESIGN BASELINE REPOSITORY	**BASELINE**	**DB**
Internal Design Phase End-Document/Repository	**Phase**	**ID**
General Statements	*ID 1st level*	*1.0*
Purpose of the Internal Design	ID 2d level	1.1
Project References	ID 2d level	1.2
Index of Programs	ID 2d level	1.3
Index of Files	ID 2d level	1.4
Index of Outputs	ID 2d level	1.5
Terms and Abbreviations	ID 2d level	1.6
Inputs and Outputs	*ID 1st level*	*2.0*
Input Document Formats	ID 2d level	2.1
Input Screen Formats	ID 2d level	2.2
Output Document Formats	ID 2d level	2.3
Output Screen Formats	ID 2d level	2.4
Data Base Specifications	*ID 1st level*	*3.0*
Data Base Summary	ID 2d level	3.1
Labeling/Tagging Conventions	ID 2d level	3.2
Data Base Organization	ID 2d level	3.3
Special Instructions	ID 2d level	3.4
File Layouts	ID 2d level	3.5
Table Layouts	ID 2d level	3.6
Record Layouts	ID 2d level	3.7
Program Specifications	*ID 1st level*	*4.0*
Support Software Environment	ID 2d level	4.1
Interfaces	ID 2d level	4.2
Storage Requirements	ID 2d level	4.3

Table 3-3. Design Baseline SCI Labeling Scheme (*Continued*)

Software Configuration Item	SCI Level	Label
DESIGN BASELINE REPOSITORY	**BASELINE**	**DB**
Program Design	ID 2d level	4.4
Detail Summary	ID 3d level	4.4.1
Logic Flow	ID 3d level	4.4.2
Initialization/Sign-on	ID 3d level	4.4.3
Operator Messages	ID 3d level	4.4.4
User Messages	ID 3d level	4.4.5
Job Setup	ID 3d level	4.4.6
Controls and Security	*ID 1st level*	*5.0*
I/O Control	ID 2d level	5.1
User Controls	ID 2d level	5.2
Data Base/File Controls	ID 2d level	5.3
Access Controls	ID 2d level	5.4
Error Controls	ID 2d level	5.5
Audit Trails	ID 2d level	5.6
Backup / Recovery Procedures	*ID 1st level*	*6.0*
Backup Procedures	ID 2d level	6.1
File Retention Procedures	ID 2d level	6.2
Restart Procedures	ID 2d level	6.3
Constraints	*ID 1st level*	*7.0*
Operating Time Window Constraints	ID 2d level	7.1
Hardware Constraints	ID 2d level	7.2
Software Constraints	ID 2d level	7.3
Communications Constraints	ID 2d level	7.4
Plans	*ID 1st level*	*8.0*
Test Plans	ID 2d level	8.1
Conversion Plans	ID 2d level	8.2
Implementation Plans	ID 2d level	8.3
Maintenance Plans	ID 2d level	8.4
Documentation Plans	ID 2d level	8.5

The project file and phase end documentation of the design baseline is illustrated in Figure 3-9.

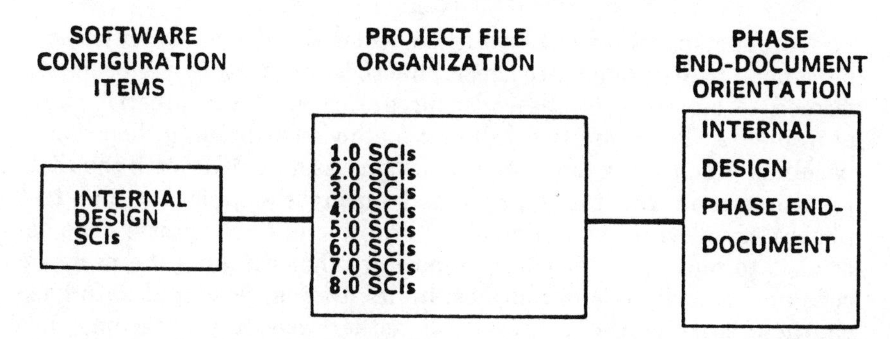

Figure 3-9. Project File/Phase End-Document Orientation of Design Baseline

The composition of the design baseline repository is illustrated in Figure 3-10.

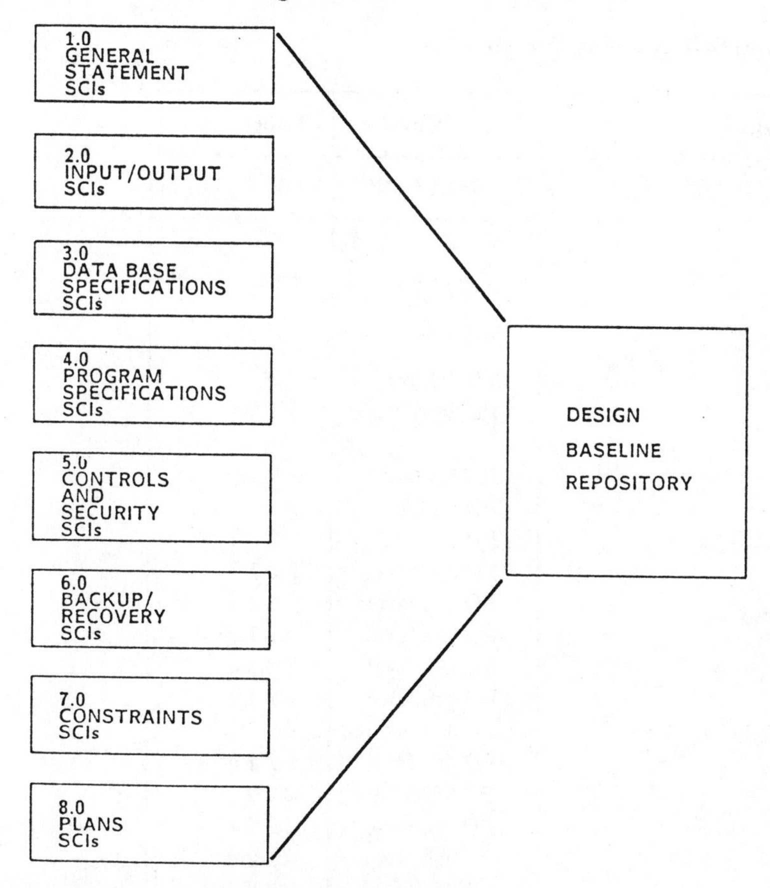

Figure 3-10. Design Baseline Repository

3.6 Task 6: Identify the Product Baseline Configuration Items

The product baseline is established when the design specifications have been transformed into executable code and testing has been performed to ensure that the coded programs meet the prescribed requirements. There are two different methods for defining the product baseline. The first is to merge the design baseline SCIs with the SCIs resulting from the tasks performed during the program and test phases of software development to form a single repository. The second is to maintain a separate repository that contains the program code and descriptions of routines, limits, timing, flow, and data base characteristics of the program. In either case, the program, once validated, establishes a baseline from which no further changes can be made to the configuration identification without initiating a formal request for software modification. The labeling scheme for identifying product baseline SCIs is outlined in Table 3-4.

Table 3-4. Product Baseline SCI Labeling Scheme

Software Configuration Item	SCI Level	Label
PRODUCT BASELINE REPOSITORY	**BASELINE**	**DB**
Program Description End-Document/Repository	**Subphase**	**PD**
General Statements	*PD 1st level*	*1.0*
Project References	PD 2d level	1.1
Requirements	*PD 1st level*	*2.0*
Subprogram Detailed Description	PD 2d level	2.1
Subprogram Data Design	PD 2d level	2.2
Arrays	PD 3d level	2.2.1
Array Name	PD 4th level	2.2.1.1
Purpose and Attributes	PD 4th level	2.2.1.2
Size and Indexing Procedure	PD 4th level	2.2.1.3
Scaling Factors	PD 4th level	2.2.1.4
Range of Values/Initial Condition	PD 4th level	2.2.1.5
Bit Layout	PD 4th level	2.2.1.6
Variables	PD 3d level	2.2.2
Variable Name	PD 4th level	2.2.2.1
Purpose and Type	PD 4th level	2.2.2.2
Size	PD 4th level	2.2.2.3

Table 3-4. Product Baseline SCI Labeling Scheme (*Continued*)

Software Configuration Item	SCI Level	Label
PRODUCT BASELINE REPOSITORY	**BASELINE**	**DB**
Range of Values/Initial Condition	PD 4th level	2.2.2.4
Bit Layout	PD 4th level	2.2.2.5
Constants	PD 3d level	2.2.3
Constant Name	PD 4th level	3.2.3.1
Purpose	PD 4th level	2.2.3.2
Initial Condition	PD 4th level	2.2.3.3
Bit Layout	PD 4th level	2.2.3.4
Flags	PD 3d level	2.2.4
Flag Name	PD 4th level	2.2.4.1
Purpose and Status	PD 4th level	2.2.4.2
Initial Condition	PD 4th level	2.2.4.3
Bit Layout	PD 4th level	2.2.4.4
Indexes	PD 3d level	2.2.5
Index Name	PD 4th level	2.2.5.1
Purpose	PD 4th level	2.2.5.2
Common Data Base Reference	PD 3d level	2.2.6
Input/Output Formats	PD 2d level	2.3
Required Library Subroutines	PD 2d level	2.4
Conditions for Initiation	PD 2d level	2.5
Subprogram Limitations	PD 2d level	2.6
Interface Description	PD 2d level	2.7
Quality Assurance Provisions	*PD 1st level*	*3.0*
Test Plan	**Subphase**	**TP**
General Statements	*TP 1st level*	*1.0*
Statement of Purpose	TP 2d level	1.1
Project References	TP 2d level	1.2
Test Schedules	TP 2d level	1.3
Testing Requirements	*TP 1st level*	*2.0*
Level of Test	TP 2d level	2.1
Functions to Be Tested	TP 2d level	2.2
Test Management Requirements	*TP 1st level*	*3.0*

Table 3-4. Product Baseline SCI Labeling Scheme (*Continued*)

Software Configuration Item	SCI Level	Label
PRODUCT BASELINE REPOSITORY	**BASELINE**	**DB**
Project Team Responsibilities	TP 2d level	3.1
Supplier Responsibilities	TP 2d level	3.2
Personnel Requirements	*TP 1st level*	*4.0*
Hardware Requirements	*TP 1st level*	*5.0*
Computer and Peripheral Equipment	TP 2d level	5.1
Interface Requirements	TP 2d level	5.2
Supporting Software Requirements	*TP 1st level*	*6.0*
Quality Assurance Procedures	*TP 1st level*	*7.0*
Test Specification	**Subphase**	**TS**
General Statements	*TS 1st level*	*1.0*
Statement of Purpose	TS 2d level	1.1
Project References	TS 2d level	1.2
Test Schedules	TS 2d level	1.3
Testing Requirements	*TS 1st level*	*2.0*
System/Program Definition	TS 2d level	2.1
List of Test Inputs	TS 3d level	2.1.1
Accuracy Requirements	TS 3d level	2.1.2
List of Required Output Values	TS 3d level	2.1.3
Data Collection Methods	TS 3d level	2.1.4
Input/Output System Interfaces	TS 3d level	2.1.5
Timing Requirements	TS 3d level	2.1.6
Display Requirements	TS 3d level	2.1.7
Communications Requirements	TS 3d level	2.1.8
Test Management Requirements	*TS 1st level*	*3.0*
Personnel Requirements	*TS 1st level*	*4.0*
Hardware Requirements	*TS 1st level*	*5.0*

Table 3-4. Product Baseline SCI Labeling Scheme (*Continued*)

Software Configuration Item	SCI Level	Label
PRODUCT BASELINE REPOSITORY	**BASELINE**	**DB**
Support Software Requirements	*TS 1st level*	*6.0*
QA Procedures	*TS 1st level*	*7.0*
Program Test Procedures	**Subphase**	**PT**
General Statements	*PT 1st level*	*1.0*
Statement of Purpose	PT 2d level	1.1
Project References	PT 2d level	1.2
General Instructions	*PT 1st level*	*2.0*
Material Requirements	PT 2d level	2.1
List of Specifications	PT 3d level	2.1.1
List of Handbooks and Manuals	PT 3d level	2.1.2
List of Machine-Readable Media	PT 3d level	2.1.3
Personnel Procedures	PT 2d level	2.2
Setup Procedures	PT 2d level	2.3
Power-on Procedures	PT 2d level	2.4
Load and Step Procedures	PT 2d level	2.5
Testing Requirements	*PT 1st level*	*3.0*
Title/Preparation Procedures	PT 2d level	3.1
Equipment Preparation Procedures	PT 3d level	3.1.1
Computer Preparation Procedures	PT 3d level	3.1.2
Testing Procedures	PT 3d level	3.1.3
Test Management Requirements	*PT 1st level*	*4.0*
Personnel Requirements	*PT 1st level*	*5.0*
Hardware Requirements	*PT 1st level*	*6.0*
Support Software Requirements	*PT 1st level*	*7.0*
QA Procedures	*PT 1st level*	*8.0*

Table 3-4. Product Baseline SCI Labeling Scheme (*Continued*)

Software Configuration Item	SCI Level	Label
PRODUCT BASELINE REPOSITORY	**BASELINE**	**DB**
Program Test Report	**Subphase**	**TR**
General Statements	*TR 1st level*	*1.0*
Statement of Purpose	TR 2d level	1.1
Project References	TR 2d level	1.2
Test Criteria	*TR 1st level*	*2.0*
Range of Data and Test Values	TR 2d level	2.1
Accuracy Requirements	TR 2d level	2.2
Program/Subprogram Capability Requirements	TR 2d level	2.3
Data Rate Requirements	TR 2d level	2.4
Test Duration Requirements	TR 2d level	2.5
Definitions of *Error* and *Failure*	TR 2d level	2.6
Test Results	*TR 1st level*	*3.0*
Evaluation Criteria	*TR 1st level*	*4.0*
Test Analysis	*TR 1st level*	*5.0*
List of Recommendations	*TR 1st level*	*6.0*
Program Package Document	**Subphase**	**PP**
Source Programs	*PP 1st level*	*1.0*
Object Programs	*PP 1st level*	*2.0*
Listings	*PP 1st level*	*3.0*
Source Listing	PP 2d level	3.1
Source/Object Listing	PP 2d level	3.2
Cross-Reference Listing	PP 2d level	3.3
Record Layouts	*PP 1st level*	*4.0*
Data Dictionary	*PP 1st level*	*5.0*

The project file and phase end-document orientation of the product baseline is illustrated in Figure 3-11.

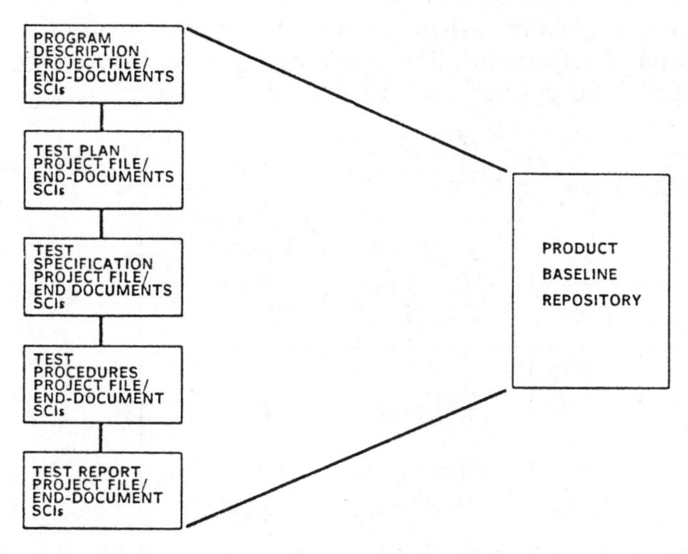

Figure 3-11. Project File/Phase End-Document Orientation of Product Baseline

Figure 3-12 illustrates the creation of the product baseline repository.

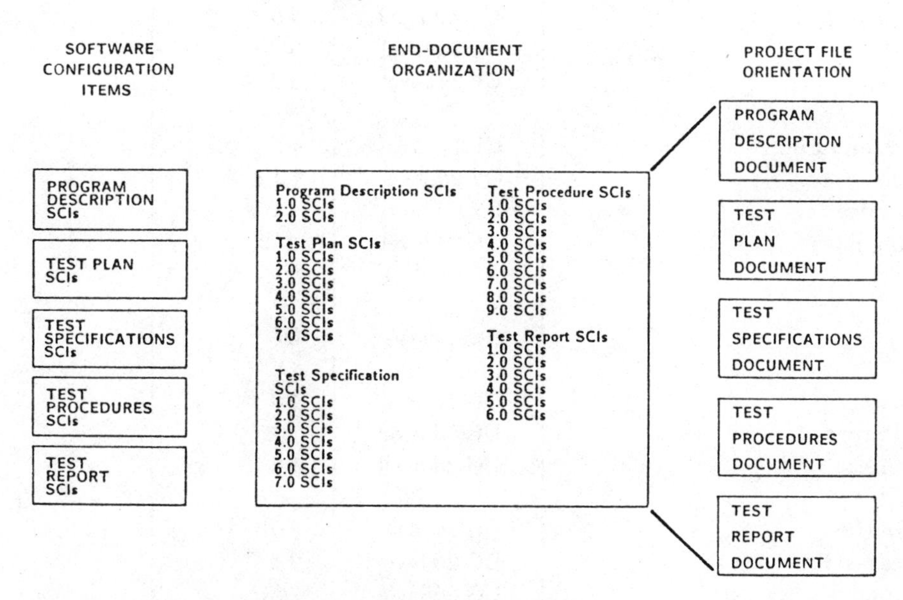

Figure 3-12. Product Baseline Repository

3.7 Task 7: Identify the Operational Baseline Configuration Items

The operational baseline is established when the conversion process is completed, and a working system is released that conforms to the requirements and specifications. The labeling scheme for identifying operational baseline SCIs is outlined in Table 3-5.

Table 3-5. Operational Baseline SCI Labeling Scheme

Software Configuration Item	SCI Level	Label
OPERATIONAL BASELINE REPOSITORY	**BASELINE**	**DB**
Conversion Documents	**Subphase**	**PP**
Conversion Plan	*CV 1st level*	*1.0*
Conversion Plan Update	CV 2d level	1.1
Conversion Plan Checklist	CV 2d level	1.2
Conversion Requirements	*CV 1st level*	*2.0*
Resources	CV 2d level	2.1
Organization	CV 2d level	2.2
Training Requirements	*CV 1st level*	*3.0*
EDP Personnel	CV 2d level	3.1
User Personnel	CV 2d level	3.2
File Conversion/Data Entry	*CV 1st level*	*4.0*
File Conversion	CV 2d level	4.1
Creating New Files	CV 3d level	4.1.1
Update Existing Files	CV 3d level	4.1.2
Users Guide	**Subphase**	**UG**
General Statements	*UG 1st level*	*1.0*
Statement of Purpose	UG 2d level	1.1
Project References	UG 2d level	1.2
Summary Statements	*UG 1st level*	*2.0*
System Application Statement	UG 2d level	2.1
System Operation	UG 2d level	2.2

Table 3-5. Operational Baseline SCI Labeling Scheme (*Continued*)

Software Configuration Item	SCI Level	Label
OPERATIONAL BASELINE REPOSITORY	**BASELINE**	**DB**
System Configuration	UG 2d level	2.3
Performance Capabilities	UG 2d level	2.4
Data Base Functions	UG 2d level	2.5
I/O Descriptions	UG 2d level	2.6
User Procedures	*UG 1st level*	*3.0*
Initiation Procedures	UG 2d level	3.1
Input Procedures	UG 2d level	3.2
Input Formats	UG 3d level	3.2.1
Composition Rules	UG 3d level	3.2.2
Output Requirements	UG 2d level	3.3
Output Formats	UG 3d level	3.3.1
Output Codes and Abbreviations	UG 3d level	3.3.2
Recovery and Error Correction Procedures	UG 2d level	3.4
File Query Procedures	*UG 1st level*	*4.0*
System Query Capabilities	UG 2d level	4.1
Data Base Format	UG 2d level	4.2
Query Preparation Procedures	UG 2d level	4.3
Run Sequence Procedures	UG 2d level	4.4
Data Retrieval Procedures	*UG 1st level*	*5.0*
Data Base Content	UG 2d level	5.1
Data Base Access Procedures	UG 2d level	5.2
Display and Retrieval Procedures	UG 2d level	5.3
Recovery and Error Correction Procedures	UG 2d level	5.4
Termination Procedures	UG 2d level	5.5
Operator's Manual	**Subphase**	**OM**
General Statements	*OM 1st level*	*1.0*
Statement of Purpose	OM 2d level	1.1
Project References	OM 2d level	1.2
Run Descriptions	*OM 1st level*	*2.0*
Run Inventory	OM 2d level	2.1

Table 3-5. Operational Baseline SCI Labeling Scheme (*Continued*)

Software Configuration Item	SCI Level	Label
OPERATIONAL BASELINE REPOSITORY	**BASELINE**	**DB**
Phasing Schedule	OM 2d level	2.2
Run Processing Procedures	OM 2d level	2.3
JCL Listings	OM 3d level	2.3.1
Management Information	OM 3d level	2.3.2
Run Identification	OM 4th level	2.3.2.1
Peripheral and Resource Requirements	OM 4th level	2.3.2.2
Security Consideration	OM 4th level	2.3.2.3
Estimated Run Time	OM 4th level	2.3.2.4
Messages and Responses	OM 4th level	2.3.2.5
Operational Standards	OM 4th level	2.3.2.6
Input/Output Files	OM 3d level	2.3.3
File Name	OM 4th level	2.3.3.1
Security Consideration	OM 4th level	2.3.3.2
Recording Medium	OM 4th level	2.3.3.3
Retention Schedule	OM 4th level	2.3.3.4
File Disposition	OM 4th level	2.3.3.5
Output Reports	OM 3d level	2.3.4
Report Identification	OM 4th level	2.3.4.1
Security and Privacy	OM 4th level	2.3.4.2
Output Medium	OM 4th level	2.3.4.3
Report Volume	OM 4th level	2.3.4.4
Number of Copies	OM 4th level	2.3.4.5
Report Distribution	OM 4th level	2.3.4.6
Report Reproduction Methods	OM 3d level	2.3.5
Report Identification	OM 4th level	2.3.5.1
Reproduction Technique	OM 4th level	2.3.5.2
Paper Size	OM 4th level	2.3.5.3
Binding Method	OM 4th level	2.3.5.4
Distribution of Copies	OM 4th level	2.3.5.5
Restart/Recovery Procedures	OM 3d level	2.3.6

As shown in Figure 3-5, the operational baseline repository consists essentially of SCIs that were produced during the implementation phase of software development and published in conversion documents, user guides, and operations manuals.

The preparation of implementation documentation is often viewed as the total sum of the software development process. In a well-defined software development environment, however, the preparation of implementation documents is essentially an iterative process that synthesizes and reorganizes document items produced during the analysis and design phases. Figure 3-13 shows the documentation sources that provide input to implementation documents and subsequently to the operational baseline for configuration management.

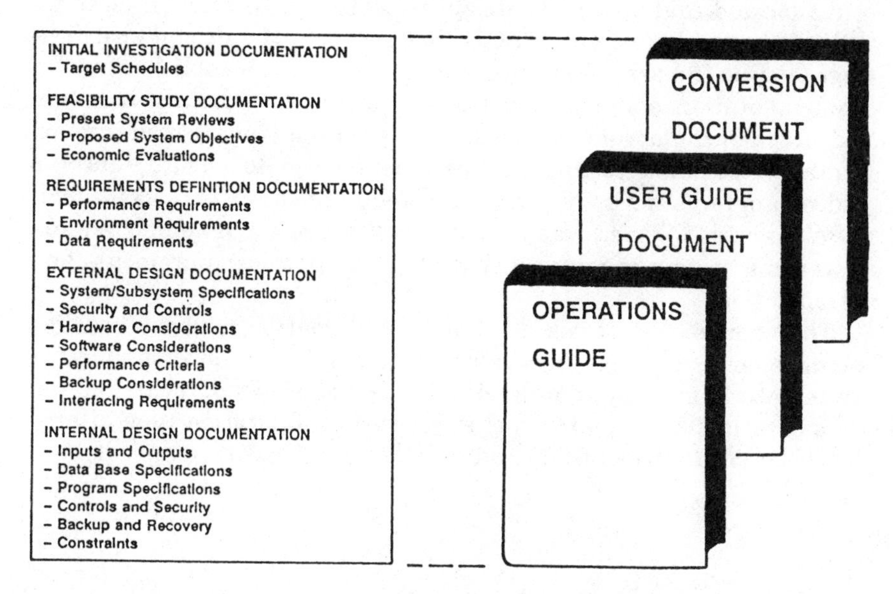

Figure 3-13. Implementation Documentation Sources

3.8 Summary

In the preceding pages we showed how the baselines for configuration control are established at various stages of the system life cycle. We illustrated how each baseline identifies the actual state of development at a given point in the software development process.

We have seen that the most elementary entity in the configuration management process is the individual software configuration item (SCI). The accumulation of SCIs at the end of each phase creates a higher-level entity that provides software managers with a central point of reference for all SCIs generated during a given phase. The SCIs derived from each phase are in turn cataloged and maintained in a baseline repository to ensure proper identification, control, status accounting, recording, filing, maintenance, safeguarding, and retrieval.

Once a baseline has been established, changes to any of the SCIs contained in the baseline repository must be processed through formal change control channels.

The baseline concept is used for configuration control through all phases of the systems development life cycle. The *functional baseline* is established when all the analysis tasks have been completed and adequately documented. The *allocated baseline* is established when the subsystems have been defined and the functional requirements are allocated to the appropriate subsystems. The *design baseline* results from the aggregate of SCIs that set forth the design specifications, define the user procedures and controls, and establish plans for implementation and maintenance. The *product baseline* is established when the design specifications have been transformed into executable code and testing has been performed to ensure that the coded programs meet the prescribed requirements. The *operational baseline* is established when the conversion process is completed and a working system is released that conforms to the requirements and specifications.

The change control board is the central control point for baseline management. Chapter 4 provides a detailed discussion related to the systematic evaluation, coordination, approval or disapproval, and implementation of all approved changes to a configuration item after it has been formally identified and included in the baseline repository.

Chapter

4

Software Configuration Control

A prime ingredient for a successful configuration management system is rigorous change control. Formal procedures are required to control changes to software configuration items (SCIs) such as inputs, outputs, and program modules. Knowing the impact a proposed change may have on costs and performance facilitates sound decisions and lends to product integrity.

Formal channels of communications must be established through all levels of the system that permit users, design personnel, and contractors to request changes to configuration items. All requests for changes must be made in writing, reviewed by representatives of the operating and design organizations, and finally approved by the change control board or other management control group. In addition, the change mechanism must ensure that all parties affected by the proposed modifications have an opportunity to comment on them before formal approval or disapproval and that change implementation schedules are established, published, and achieved.

Changes in the configuration identification must be documented accurately and concurrently with the implementation of the change. The steps involved in the processing of changes to the configuration identification are outlined below.

1. The user, designer, or contractor detects a discrepancy in the system design or determines a change in requirement which requires a change to one or more configuration items.
2. The concerned party prepares a discrepancy report or a software

change request and submits it to the configuration manager.
3. The configuration manager reviews the proposed modification, numbers it for tracking purposes, logs the request, determines the change classification, and places the request on the agenda of the change control board.
4. The CCB reviews the request and agrees or disagrees with the request. If the CCB agrees with the request, a technical and business assessment of the proposed change is conducted.
5. Reports of these assessments are presented to the CCB. If satisfied that the change is beneficial, the CCB signs off on the request and it is tracked through the normal control procedures.

Software configuration control evolves from the baselines that establish the configuration identification. The tasks involved in developing the configuration control methodology are shown in Figure 4-1 and detailed on the following pages.

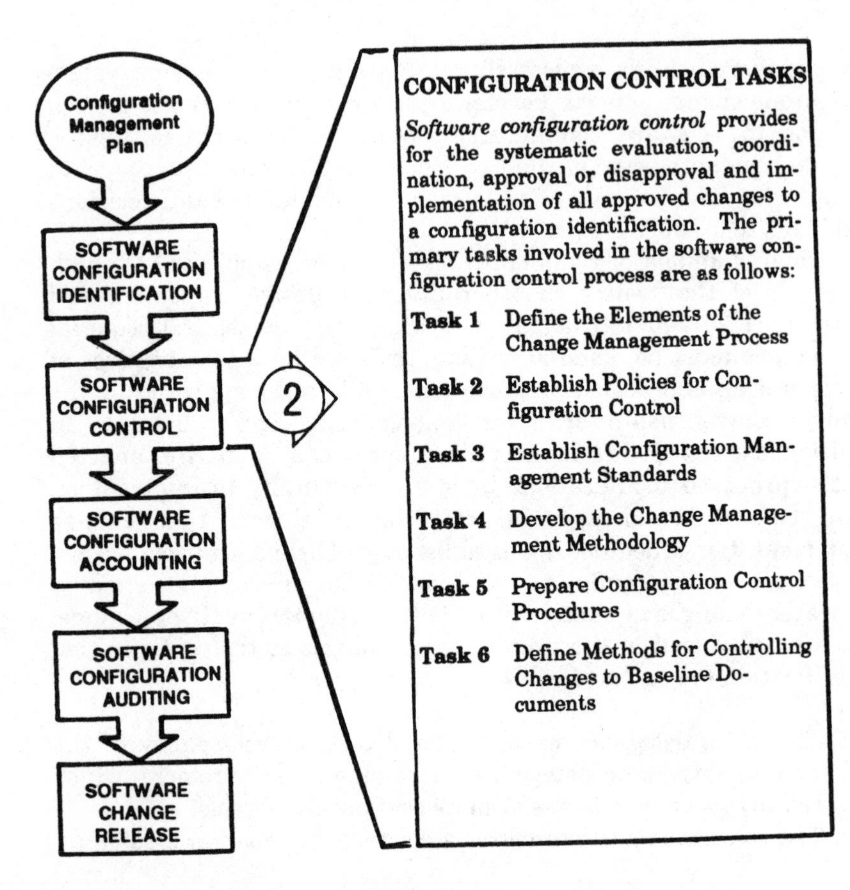

Figure 4-1. Software Configuration Control Tasks

4.1 Task 1: Define the Elements of the Change Management Process

The first step in the software configuration control process is to design and implement a methodology that breaks the work to be performed into functional elements. The front-to-back sequencing of these elements will enable a request for change to be tracked from the time it is initiated until the change is installed. The elements of the change control methodology are shown in Table 4-1.

Table 4-1. Elements of a Change Control Methodology

Element	Purpose
Change initiation	To establish a protocol for requesting changes to configuration items for which identification has been established
Technical evaluation	To establish a protocol for evaluating the risk and technical feasibility of implementing a change request
Business evaluation	To establish a protocol to ensure that the requested change and timing of the proposed change are compatible to the company's goals.
Management review	To establish a protocol of evaluating the technical and business recommendations and approving or disapproving a change request
Test tracking	To establish a protocol for monitoring test results and test progress
Installation tracking	To establish a protocol for monitoring the installation progress of all changes to configuration items
Formal qualification	To establish a protocol for verifying that the modified baseline performs properly in a production environment

In addition, the methodology must consider a change coordination activity that provides a central point for directing and monitoring the status of each change request. The change coordination activity is essential to ensure the administration and surveillance of the change process.

4.2 Task 2: Establish Policies for Configuration Control

The change control process begins by defining policy. An understanding of the company's philosophy and goals relative to software configuration management should be clearly expressed. The publication of these policies in a formal policy manual provides a mechanism through which the company's philosophy and objectives relative to configuration control can be promulgated and made operative. In the broad context, configuration policies should be written and published that establish the framework for:

- Assignment of responsibility and authority for configuration control
- Monitoring, auditing, and reviewing changes to configuration items
- Defining the baseline contents
- Defining the format and content of the phase end-documents
- Establishing procedures to facilitate traceability of changes to configuration identifications
- Defining the elements of configuration control
- Developing guidelines for configuration accounting
- Conducting periodic audits and monitoring actions to ensure compliance with specifications and standards
- Identifying the organizational elements responsible for testing the configuration items that comprise the configuration identification

Examples of policy statements for each element are provided below and on the following pages.

Define Change Initiation Policy. A change initiation policy will ensure consistency in the way change requests are prepared and submitted to the CCB for review and approval. The purpose of such a policy is not to prescribe step-by-step procedures for initiating change requests, but rather to convey policy information pertaining to types of changes to be controlled; change control board functions; requirements for initiating, communicating, recording, and tracking change requests; document flow between the requestor and the CCB; and time-cycle requirements.

Example:

PURPOSE
The purpose of the change initiation element of the change management system is to establish a protocol for requesting changes to configuration items for which identification has been established.

OBJECTIVES
The objectives of the change initiation protocol are:

- To establish a consistent approach to initiating change requests
- To define the communication and control responsibilities of the change control board (CCB)

POLICIES

1. The types of changes to be controlled by the change system must be identified and documented.
2. The characteristics of each change category must be defined and documented.
3. The activities needed for each category must be defined and documented.
4. The review and approval flow of change request data must be defined and documented.
5. The time-cycle requirements for responding to change requests must be defined and documented.

Define Technical Assessment Policy. A technical assessment policy is needed to promote and ensure technical completeness of proposed changes. Policy statements in this category should address impacts on hardware/software, staff training requirements, vendor support requirements, program support requirements; scheduling; testing requirements, backup/Recovery requirements, and audit/security requirements.

Example:

PURPOSE
The purpose of the technical assessment element of the change management system is to establish a protocol for evaluating the risks and technical feasibility of implementing a change request.

OBJECTIVE
The objective of the technical assessment protocol is to promote and ensure technical completeness and installability of proposed changes.

POLICIES

1. All change requests must be subjected to a technical assessment.
2. A plan must be prepared for identifying data, staff, and tools required to perform the technical assessment functions.
3. Procedures must be developed for administering the technical assessment process.

Define Business Assessment Policy. A business assessment policy will ensure that the timing of proposed changes is compatible with business goals. The topics addressed in policy statements related to business assessment considerations may include categories/types of changes, change requests methods and procedures, performance indicators, tracking status of change requests, authorized approvers, and change coordinator responsibilities.

Example:

PURPOSE
The purpose of the business assessment element of the change management system is to establish a protocol to ensure that the timing of proposed changes is compatible with the company's business goals.

OBJECTIVES
The objectives of the business assessment protocol are to provide a methodology for conducting the business assessment, establish procedures for approving changes, and provide guidance in formalizing management recommendations.

POLICIES

1. Procedures must be established to facilitate the monitoring schedules and to identify timing conflicts which may exist between business and change processing activities.
2. Procedures must be established to ensure that all concerned individuals are made aware of the status of changes to configuration items.

Define Approval Policy. The function of an approval policy is to provide management with a basis for evaluating the recommendations resulting from the technical and business assessments and approving or disapproving a change request. Policy statements in this category should address the following topics type/category of changes to be reviewed, change schedules, responsibility for overall management approval, and performance indicators.

Example:

PURPOSE
The purpose of the approval element of the change management system is to establish a protocol for evaluating technical and business recommendations and approving or disapproving a change request.

OBJECTIVES
The objectives of the management approval protocol are to establish change priorities, eliminate disagreements related to the implementation of change configuration, and establish procedures for approving/disapproving or delaying proposed changes to configuration items.

POLICIES

1. Procedures must be established for prioritizing and scheduling changes.
2. Forms or reports must be designed that reflect the management approval activity.
3. Staff assignments and individual responsibilities must be defined for change approval and processing.
4. The format of management review meetings must be established.
5. Procedures for monitoring all changes approved for test must be developed.
6. Arbitration or escalation processes must be defined.

Define Test Tracking Policy. A test tracking policy establishes the framework for monitoring test results to ensure that changes are tested in a consistent manner. Policy statements in this category should address test environment requirements, stress levels, reporting procedures, responsibilities for testing, and performance indicators.

Example:

PURPOSE
The purpose of the test tracking element of the change management system is to establish a protocol for monitoring test results and test progress.

OBJECTIVE
The objective of the test tracking protocol is to ensure that the testing process adheres to testing standards and schedules as set forth in the test plan.

POLICIES

1. Procedures must be established for tracking changes to host computer hardware, remote hardware, host software, communications equipment, and facilities.
2. Standards and guidelines must be established for monitoring and controlling test activities.

Installation Tracking Policy. The objective of an installation tracking policy is to ensure that the installations of all changes adhere to established standards. change plans, and procedures. The topics addressed may include daily change schedules, weekly change schedules, and concurrent changes in hardware, software, and application environments.

Example:

PURPOSE
The purpose of the installation tracking element of the change management system is to monitor the installation progress of all changes to configuration items.

OBJECTIVES
The objectives of the installation tracking protocol are to ensure that all standards are adhered to when installing changes and to monitor the effectiveness of all installation activities.

POLICIES

1. A master calendar that provides an overview of changes to be installed over an extended period of time must be maintained.
2. A master calendar that shows the changes to be implemented over the next biweekly period shall be prepared on a weekly basis.
3. A mechanism for providing an overview of the planned evolution of the configuration shall be developed for each monthly period.
4. Establish guidelines for processing concurrent changes in the hardware, software, and application environments.

5. Define the types and contents of logs required to maintain control of remote stations.

Change Coordination Policy. The objective of a change coordination policy is to provide for central direction and monitoring of the change management process.

Example:

PURPOSE
The purpose of the change coordination element of the change management system is to define the required coordination activities to manage all changes to configuration items.

OBJECTIVES
The objectives of the change coordination element are to ensure that all change proposals are efficiently handled and that all practical steps are taken to ensure that changes are implemented without disruption of the business functions.

POLICIES
The change coordination entity shall:

- Provide central direction and monitoring of all elements of the change management system
- Publish instructions to those who will be requesting changes
- Act as a focal point for complaints and suggestions about the change system
- Act as the decision maker for the data processing management in all matters concerning changes to the configuration identification
- Maintain a change management library
- Verify that changes are properly entered into the data base
- Assemble change and problem history records
- Revise procedures if appropriate
- Maintain a calendar of approved changes
- Act as a focal point for complaints
- Provide technical advice on change techniques

4.3 Task 3: Establish Configuration Management Standards

Having defined the configuration control policies and procedures, our next task is to establish standards that will control the overall configuration management process. Generally, standards should be adopted that provide technical and administrative direction to:

- Identify and document the functional and physical characteristics of a configuration item
- Control changes to those characteristics
- Record and report change processing and implementation status

Specifically, the following types of standards should be established to guide the overall software configuration management action:

- Configuration management plan (CMP) standards establish the formats, contents, and procedures for the preparation of a configuration management plan.
- Baseline management standards provide guidelines for the development and revision of baseline documents.
- Interface control standards set forth criteria and guidance for documentation and control of all physical and functional interfaces.
- Configuration identification standards relate to the identification of software configuration items including standards that prescribe a numbering scheme for identifying SCIs.
- Change control standards provide criteria for the systematic evaluation, coordination, approval or disapproval, and implementation of changes to configuration items.
- Release requirement standards establish guidelines for the control of the initial releases and subsequent revision of documentation and media.
- Configuration audit standards establish criteria for validating the functional and physical configurations of a configuration item.
- Configuration accounting standards apply to the recording and reporting of the information needed to manage a configuration effectively.

Configuration Management Plan Standards. The configuration management plan is a document that outlines the procedures for configuration identification, control, accounting, and auditing. It also defines the responsibilities of the various persons or groups designated to implement the procedures.

Example:

PURPOSE
This standard provide guidelines for the development and revision of a configuration management plan (CMP) that outlines the procedures and assigns responsibility for configuration identification, control, auditing, and accounting.

SCOPE
This standard establishes the formats, contents, and procedures for the preparation of a CMP and changes thereto.

DEFINITIONS
The key terms used in this standard are defined as follows:

Configuration Accounting. The recording and reporting of information that is needed to manage configuration effectively, including a listing of the approved configuration identification, the status of proposed changes to configuration, and the implementation of approved changes.
Configuration Auditing. The mechanism for determining the degree to which the current state of a software development effort coincides with the requirements documentation.
Configuration Control. The systematic evaluation, coordination, approval or disapproval, and implementation of all approved changes to a configuration item.
Configuration Identification. The current approved or conditionally approved technical documentation for a configuration item.
Configuration Management. A discipline applying technical and administrative direction and surveillance to identify configuration items and control changes to the configuration identification.
Configuration Management Plan. A project document which describes the requirements for configuration management, the procedures to be followed in making changes to configuration items, and the persons/groups responsible for each particular phase of configuration management.

STANDARDS

1. **Front Matter**. Unless otherwise specified, material preceding the first text page shall consist of the following:

Cover. The cover of the CMP shall contain information noting the project to which the CMP applies and the date of issue of the CMP.
Title page. Unless otherwise stated by the configuration manager, the information on the title page shall be the same as the information on the cover.
Foreword/Preface. A foreword or preface shall contain the purpose and scope of the CMP.
Table of contents. A table of contents listing sections and subsections of the CMP shall be placed at the beginning of each section.

2. **Content Arrangement**. The CMP shall contain eight numbered sections, titled and numbered as shown below:

1.0 Scope. The statement of the scope shall present a clear, concise abstract of the scope of the CMP and may include, whenever necessary, information as to the use of the CMP.

2.0 Reference Documents. This section of the CMP is used to list those documents that should be referenced to support the configuration management process.

3.0 Organization. This section shall describe the relationship of configuration management to functional organizations.

4.0 Interface Control. This section shall provide general guidance for determining the requirements for the control of interfaces.

5.0 Configuration Identification. This section shall explain the documentation requirements for a currently approved or conditionally approved configuration item. It should also explain the configuration item numbering system used to identify an SCI.

6.0 Change Control. This section shall explain the procedures and reference standards that pertain to the systematic evaluation, coordination, approval or disapproval, and implementation of changes to configuration items.

7.0 Configuration Status Accounting. This section shall define the requirements for recording and reporting of information needed to manage configuration effectively.

8.0 Configuration Auditing. This section shall summarize or reference those standards that establish criteria for validating the functional and physical configurations of a configuration item.

Subject matter shall be kept within the scope of the sections so that the same kind of requirements or information will always appear in the same section of every CMP. If there is no information pertinent to a section, the following shall appear below the section heading: *This section is not applicable to this CMP.*

Baseline Management Standards. Baseline management is the application of administrative direction to designate the documents and changes thereto which formally identify, designate, and control the configuration identification of a software product. An example of a baseline management standard is shown below and on the next page.

Example:

PURPOSE
This standard designates the baseline documents which establish the configuration identification at specific stages of the software development process and provides guidelines for content development for each baseline document.

SCOPE
This standard provides guidance for the development and revision of functional baseline, allocated baseline, design baseline, product baseline, and operational baseline documents.

DEFINITIONS
The key terms used in this standard are defined as follows:

Allocated Baseline. The document or set of documents that define the functions to be performed by the software and hardware.
Baseline. A document, or set of documents, that establishes the configuration identification at certain stages of development.
Baseline Management. The process of administering the identification, designation, and control of configuration items at specific points in the software development life cycle.
Design Baseline. The document or set of documents which defines the means of controlling and assessing the integrity of all software components to be coded.
Product Baseline. The document or set of documents that represent the working product, including source listings, object listings, cross-reference listings, and test reports.
Operational Baseline. The document or set of documents that includes the response to product testing and serves as release documents for the working system.
Software Configuration Item (SCI). Any of the discrete portions of software components which satisfy an end-use function.

STANDARDS

1. **Baseline Identification.** The baseline identifications to be established for each MIS project shall be as follows:

   - Functional baseline
   - Allocated baseline
   - Design baseline
   - Product baseline
   - Operational baseline

2. **Document Types.** The document types that comprise each baseline shall be as follows:

Functional baseline documents
- Initial investigation
- Feasibility study
- Requirements definition

Allocated baseline document
- External design

Design baseline document
- Internal design

Product baseline documents
- Program package
- Test report

Operational baseline documents
- User manual
- Operation guide

3. **Initial Investigation Configuration Items.** The first-level SCIs that comprise the initial investigation document are as follows:

   - Problem and need statement
   - Cost projection
   - Feasibility study work plan

4. **Feasibility Study Configuration Items.** The first-level SCIs that comprise the feasibility study document are as follows:

- Present system documentation
- Proposed system requirements
- Comparisons of available packages

5. **Requirements Definition Configuration Items**. The first-level SCIs that comprise the requirements definition document are as follows:

- Performance requirements
- Environment requirements
- Data requirements

6. **External Design Configuration Items**. The first-level SCIs that comprise the external design document are as follows:

- System/subsystem specifications
- Security and controls
- Interfacing requirements

7. **Internal Design Configuration Items.** The first-level SCIs that comprise the internal design document are as follows:

- Inputs and outputs
- Data-base specifications
- Program specifications
- Backup/recovery procedures

8. **Test Plan Configuration Items.** The first-level SCIs that comprise the test plan document are as follows:d

- Test requirements
- Personnel requirements
- Hardware requirements
- Software requirements
- Test schedules
- QA procedures

9. **Test Specification Configuration Items**. The first-level SCIs that comprise the test plan document are as follows:

- Unit test specifications
- Module integration test specifications
- System test specifications

10. **Test Procedure Configuration Items**. The first-level SCIs that comprise the test procedure document are as follows:

- Setup procedures
- Test operating procedures

11. **Test Report Configuration Items**. The first-level SCIs that comprise the test report document are as follows:

- Test criteria statements
- Test results
- Evaluation criteria
- Tecommendations

12. **Program Package Configuration Items**. The first- and second-level SCIs that comprise the program package document are as follows:

- Program descriptions
- File descriptions

- File usage
- File layouts
- Summary documents
- Program index
- File index
- Output index
- Source program listings
- Source/object listings

Interface Control Standards. Interface control is the process by which technical agreements between two or more design activities are generated and administered. An interface control standard provides guidance for the documentation and control of all physical and functional interfaces.

An example of an interface control standard is shown below and on the next page.

Example:

PURPOSE
This standard sets forth criteria for the establishment of interface control of all physical and functional interfaces.

SCOPE
This standard provides guidance for documentation and control of systems, programs, facilities, and installation interfaces.

DEFINITIONS
Acquisition Life Cycle. The path through which all acquired programs must flow (e.g., conceptual, validation, development, production, and deployment).

Interface Control. This is the process by which agreements between two or more design activities are generated and administered.

Interface Working Control Group (ICWG). This is the entity that serves as the communication link between development personnel and the user.

STANDARDS

1. **General Guidelines**. Unless otherwise specified, interface control shall be implemented pursuant to the following guidelines.

   - The configuration manager shall determine the requirements for interface control during the validation phase of development.
   - The interface control manager shall be responsible for developing configuration identification.
   - Programs entering the acquisition phase are broken into two categories: programs requiring a hardware/computer program development cycle and programs requiring a total development cycle.
   - The establishment of an ICWG shall be specified by a request for proposal and the subsequent determination of the following: the designation of a chairperson who shall be responsible for coordinating the interface control functions, the delineation of responsibilities for interface control, and the delineation of responsibilities for status accounting and reporting.

- The relationships, responsibilities, and requirements of the interface control units shall be specified in a statement of work.

2. **Interface Control Working Group (ICWG).** The organization, responsibilities and functional requirements of the ICWG shall be as follows:

- The ICWG shall serve as the communication link between the MIS organization and the contract organization to resolve interface problems, document interface agreements, and coordinate change requests.
- The ICWG shall consist of representatives from both the MIS and Contractor organizations.
- The establishment of interface control shall require the identification and definition of interfaces, preparation, approval, release, and control of all configuration items.

3. **Interface Control Document.** An interface control document must be prepared for each system development project. The content arrangement shall be as follows:

1.0 Scope. The statement of the scope shall present a clear, concise abstract of the scope of the interface control document and may include, whenever necessary, information as to the use of the document.

2.0 Reference Documents. This section of the interface control document is used to list those documents that should be referenced to support the interface control process.

3.0 Organization. This section shall describe the relationship of interface control working group to the overall configuration management organization.

4.0 Interface Requirements. This section shall define the following:

- Data base requirements necessary to support the interface
- Special requirements (e.g., interface reliability, stability, and restrictions)
- Traceability requirements

5.0 Interface Design. This section shall describe the functions to be performed by each interface.

6.0 Quality Assurance Provisions. This section shall detail the QA considerations for interface control. It shall explain the following:

- The responsibility and authority of the interface control QA group
- Review procedures related to interface control
- Alternatives to formal QA

Configuration Identification Standards. Configuration identification is the process by which software configuration items are identified for configuration control and version tracking. An example of a configuration identification standard is shown below and on the following page.

Example:

PURPOSE
This standard establishes criteria for identifying configuration items, controlling changes to the identification, and maintaining version integrity and traceability throughout the software life cycle.

SCOPE
This standard provides guidance for defining control units, labeling configuration items, and maintaining a version register.

DEFINITIONS
The key terms used in this standard are defined as follows:

Configuration Identification. The current approved or conditionally approved technical documentation for a configuration item.
Configuration Item. Any of the discrete portions of software components which satisfy an end user.
Configuration Item Numbering. The number assigned to identify a configuration item.

STANDARDS

1. *Functional Configuration Identification.* Specifications governing the identification of functional configuration items must prescribe:

   - Required functional characteristics
   - Required interface controls
   - First-level and key lower-level configuration items
   - Design constraints of configuration items

2. *Allocated Configuration Identification.* Specifications governing the identification of allocated configuration items must:

   - Define the allocation of functional characteristics among first-level configuration items
   - Establish the requirements for testing the functional characteristics of the configuration items
   - Delineate interface requirements
   - Establish design constraints

3. *Product Configuration Identification.* Documentation which defines the product configuration identification must include:

   - Physical characteristics of each configuration item
   - Functional characteristics considered for production acceptance testing
   - Production test criteria

4. *Item Identification Numbers.* Identification numbers to be used for configuration management shall be as follows:

   - Specification or standard number
   - Configuration item number
   - Change identification number
   - Registration number
   - Computer program number
   - Version description document number

5. *Traceability.* The procedures for tracking configuration items from inception and initial release through the various versions shall consider the following:

- Changes to tapes, decks, or disks
- Traceability of program patches
- Changes to source programs
- Changes in control documentation

6. *Version Description Document.* Specifications pertaining to the preparation of version description documents shall consider the following:

   - The identification of the physical media of a program
   - An inventory of each type of physical medium.
   - A list of changes that have been incorporated in the configuration identification
   - The interface capabilities
   - Installation instructions

Change Control Standards. Change control is the process by which modifications and/or additions to a configuration item are managed. An example of a change control standard is shown here and on the following page.

Example:

PURPOSE
This standard defines the general flow of configuration changes and establishes responsibilities for change control through the various elements of the configuration management system.

SCOPE
This standard defines the elements of the change management system and outlines the activities for each change processing element.

DEFINITIONS
Business Evaluation. The process by which the proposed change is evaluated in terms of workloads, budgetary constraints, and corporate goals.
Change Initiation. The process through which a change request is introduced.
Install Tracking. The process by which the installation progress and changes to all configuration items are monitored and tracked.
Management Approval. The process by which technical and business recommendations are approved or disapproved.
Technical Evaluation. The process by which the risks and technical feasibility of implementing a change request are evaluated.
Test Tracking. The process by which test results and test progress are tracked.

STANDARDS

1. **Change Types.** The types of changes are identified as follows:

   - Hardware changes (e.g., engineering changes, equipment upgrades, terminal moves, microcode changes, etc.)
   - Software changes (e.g., enhancements, emergency changes, new releases and conversions, data set changes, and procedural changes)
   - Application program changes (e.g., new releases, data base changes, control language changes, etc.)
   - Network changes (e.g., node name and path changes, new release and conversions, spool device changes, etc.)
   - Environment changes (e.g., electrical, workspace, etc.)

- Procedure changes

2. **Change Management Activities**. The minimum activities to be performed for each element of the change management system are as follows:

   - Change initiation element
     - Prepare a change request form.
     - Classify the change request.
     - Submit the change request for management review and approval.
     - Assign a number identifying the change request.
     - Record the request in the change control log.
   - Technical assessment element
     - Review the change request to determine the impacts on the operating environment.
     - Prepare a statement of technical feasibility.
     - Prepare a technical risk statement.
   - Business assessment element
     - Review the change request to evaluate the business risk potential and effect on installation timing.
     - Prepare a statement of business risk.
     - Prepare a statement installation timing impacts.
     - Prepare a statement of benefits.
   - Management approval element
     - Accept, reject, or defer the change based on the business and technical assessments.
     - Update the change control log.
   - Test tracking element
     - Verify that the specified tests have been performed.
     - Document the results of the testing.
     - Evaluate the test results.
     - Accept, reject, or defer the change based on the test evaluations.
     - Update the change control log.
   - Install tracking element
     - Verify that the installation activity is scheduled.
     - Notify all affected parties of the pending installation schedule.
     - Make any changes to the configuration identification that may be required.
     - Update the change control log to reflect the installation of change to configuration items.

Release Requirement Standards. Release requirement standards establish the framework for version control of the initial configuration item release and subsequent revisions incorporated into the software and documentation. An example of a release requirement standard is shown below and on the following page.

Example:

PURPOSE
This standard defines the minimum requirements for the release of configuration items.

SCOPE
This standard establishes criteria for the preparation and maintenance of all software release records.

DEFINITIONS

Release Control. The procedures implemented to ensure the control of the initial release and subsequent revision of the documentation and media related to a specific configuration item.

Revision. The release or re-release of a configuration item and/or related documentation.

Version. The initial release or re-release of a computer program configuration item.

STANDARDS

The MIS organization shall maintain release documents for all configuration items in accord with the following formats and procedures.

1. **Functional Capabilities**. The recording requirements and functional capabilities of the release system shall be as follows:

   - Configuration identification numbering
     - Version number
     - Release number
     - Project ID number
     - Media ID number
     - 1st and subsequent level SCI numbers
   - Functional capabilities of release documentation
     - Identification of all levels of a configuration item (i.e., 1st level, 2d level, etc.)
     - Poject, program, subsystem, and unit identification
     - Release number and version identification
     - All class I and class II software changes released for production shall be identified by identification numbers and shall be completely released prior to formal release of the configuration item.
     - The configuration released for each configuration item at the time of its formal acceptance shall be retained in release records for a time period specified by the configuration manager.

2. **Version Integrity**. Version integrity must be maintained by controlling the construction of each version and by conducting integrity checks of the program code prior to release.

   - Version construction
     - The version construction process shall be performed by the CPL.
     - A master copy of each software version shall be maintained by the CPL.
   - Integrity checks
     - Data checks must be conducted to ensure that the program code and data base files have not changed since the product baseline was established.
     - Regression tests must be performed on each new version before formal verification.
   - Traceability
     - Changes to tapes, disks, decks, etc. must be traceable to the change request that initiated the change.
     - Changes to source programs shall be identifiable in terms of lines, cards, etc. which differ from previous versions.
     - Changes to controlled documentation shall be traceable to the code or instruction change specified in the change initiation function.

Software Configuration Audit Standards. Configuration audit standards define the products of functional and physical configuration audits, and the relationship of these audits to other review processes. An example of a configuration audit standard is shown below and on the following page.

Example:

PURPOSE
This standard sets forth the objectives to be accomplished at each of the configuration audits.

SCOPE
This standard provides general guidance for the conduct of both functional and physical configuration audits and defines the product of each audit.

DEFINITIONS
Functional Configuration Audit. An audit conducted to verify the completion or extent of completion of all tests required by the development specifications.
Physical Configuration Audit. An audit conducted to verify the documentation which establishes the product baseline for a configuration item.

STANDARDS
Functional and physical audits shall be conducted for all configuration items in accord with the following standards:

1. **User Organization Participation.** The responsibilities of the user organization in the conduct of configuration audits shall be as follows:

   - The user manager will acknowledge that a particular audit will be held and establish the extent to which the user personnel will participate.
   - The user manager will formally acknowledge the accomplishment of each audit and notify the MIS manager of the requirements for post review action. This notification will be accomplished within 10 working days after receipt of the review minutes from the MIS manager.
   - The user manager shall designate a co-chairperson.
   - The user manager will formally acknowledge the successful completion of the physical configuration audit.
2. **MIS Organization Participation.** The responsibilities of the MIS organization in the conduct of configuration audits shall be as follows:

   - The MIS manager shall propose the time, place, and agenda for each audit of each configuration item.
   - The schedule for each audit shall be established in relation to the overall program schedule.
   - The MIS manager shall designate a co-chairperson.
3. **Functional Configuration Audit (FCA).** The FCA shall encompass the following:

   - The configuration item audited shall be directly compared with the development specification requirements.
   - Differences shall be made a matter of record and reflected in the minutes of the FCA.
   - Performance analysis data and failure modes and effects

analysis data shall be reviewed to establish achievement of a specified performance parameter through test data.

- The validity of acceptance requirements shall be verified by direct comparison of the test methods and test data for the deliverable configuration item.
- Configuration items that do not require qualification testing shall have all requirements in the development specification verified during the FCA.
- The MIS manager, in cooperation with the user manager, shall develop at the conclusion of the FCA, a checklist for the conduct of the physical configuration audit (PCA) that identifies the documentation and hardware that will be available and the tasks to be accomplished.

4. **Physical Configuration Audit.** The PCA shall verify the documentation which establishes the product baseline. The PCA shall encompass the following:

- The PCA shall be conducted jointly by the user and MIS organizations.
- The user organization reserves the prerogative to have representatives of the user organization accomplish all or any portion of the required audits, inspections, and tests.
- The configuration of the configuration item audited shall be compared to the product specification.
- Item numbers and identification markings shall be compared directly with version description documents.
- Differences between the technical description contained in the product specification shall be documented in the minutes of the PCA.
- The compatibility of the detail design of the configuration item with other interfacing systems shall be established by comparison of released software data to the product audited.
- Computer program descriptive documentation contained in the product specification shall have all approved changes incorporated.
- The MIS organization's software release system and change control procedures shall be reviewed and validated against the requirements.

Configuration Accounting Standards. Configuration accounting standards provide the basis for the recording and tracking of configuration items and change status. An example of a configuration accounting standard is shown below and on the following page.

Example:

PURPOSE

This standard establishes the protocols for (1) preparing and maintaining records that are required by the change management organization to track the status of a configuration item, and (2) for reporting the status of a configuration item to the project team and the user.

SCOPE

This standard covers the preparation of all logs and status reports required to trace the evolution of the current status of a configuration item from the time of its initial release.

DEFINITIONS
The key terms used in this standard are defined as follows:

Logs. Records prepared and maintained by the configuration management organization for the purpose of monitoring the status of all configuration items.
Reports. Documents prepared to inform project personnel and the user regarding the status of configuration items.

STANDARDS
The configuration accounting system shall consist of the following logs and reports.

1. **Logs.** The following logs must be prepared:

    - A product log that lists and describes the various media, source listings, object listings, and cross-reference listings
    - A routine log that tracks the development of a software routine
    - A problem report log that provides a record of all software problem reports submitted on a particular configuration item
    - A software modification report log that provides a record of all modification reports submitted on a particular configuration item
    - A design problem report log that provides a record of all design problem reports submitted on a particular configuration item
    - A document update transmittal log that provides a record of all document update transmittal forms forwarded to the CPL
    - A specification change notice log that provides a record of all specification change notices submitted on a particular configuration item
    - A software change proposal log that provides a record of all software change proposals and related software problem reports submitted on a particular configuration item
    - A data base change request log that provides a record of all data base change requests submitted to the data base administrator
    - A test status log that provides a record of all test status reports submitted on a particular configuration item
    - A site installation log that identifies each site where software is installed and the software version at that site

2. **Reports.** The following reports must be prepared:

    - Computer program library transmittal form to accompany all code and data base information transmitted to the CPL
    - Computer program library inventory report
    - Test status report
    - Change status report
    - Specification change notice
    - Software problem status report
    - Software modification report

3. **Version Description Document.** A version description document shall be prepared that contains the following information:

    - Program name and part number identification
    - Adaptation date
    - Media identification
    - A list of all changes incorporated into the program
    - Interface compatibility
    - Installation instructions
    - Possible problems/known errors

4.4 Task 4: Develop the Change Management Methodology

Once policy has been defined and the standards for change management have been established, the next step is develop a change management methodology (CMM). The development cycle of a CMM revolves around the five major functions that encompass a typical systems development process:

- Analyze the requirements
- Design the system
- Program the design
- Test the programs
- Inplement the system

These basic functions are further subdivided into eight elements that form the change management methodology (CMM). Details about each of these elements are provided below and on the following pages.

Change Initiation Element. This element of the CMM focuses on defining procedures for initiating a change request and promulgating plans to change a baseline identification.

The process of analyzing requirements for initiating a request for change begins by gathering information needed to assess the current change initiation process. This involves obtaining sample copies of existing change request forms and collecting documentation that identifies the scope of the existing change system. The collected documents are then analyzed to determine if the current system is adequate for future needs, if the data on existing change request forms satisfies the change management needs, and if the form contains all essential fields for processing a proposed change. In addition, the data is reviewed to evaluate the current system of categorizing changes, determining lead time requirements, projecting the volumes and types of changes that can be made, and the number of changes that are presently made without proper documentation. When the analysis is completed, the findings should be documented in a change initiation requirements definition end-document that defines the requirements for initiating a change request that would alter the status of a baseline identification.

The process of designing a change initiation methodology begins by reviewing the change initiation requirements definition end-document. The tasks prescribed by the methodology may be categorized as follows: external design tasks and internal design tasks. The external design tasks focus on identifying the types of changes to be controlled, defining the change categories, determining at what point changes may be entered into the system, specifying how the requests will be entered into the system (e.g., entered on-line or manually), defining the points of collection, and identifying the data bases for entering a change request. The internal design tasks are concerned with defining the types of data needed on the change request, designing the change request form, formalizing methods for approving a change request, determining whether organizational or staffing changes are needed, and outlining a general plan for change implementation. The results of the both the external and internal design effort should be thoroughly documented and published in a change initiation design document is prepared. This document establishes the design framework for the change initiation element of the CMM.

The tasks involved in implementing the change initiation element of the CMM include finalizing and printing the change request form, writing procedures, training user and development personnel, and introducing the change request forms and procedures into the working environment.

Technical Evaluation Element. The technical assessment element of the CMM focuses on assessing the technical feasibility and technical risks of a proposed change to a configuration baseline.

The requirements definition phase begins by gathering information needed to evaluate existing mechanisms for conducting a technical assessment. The first step is to collect reports and minutes that record proceedings of the change control board or other change coordination entities. The next step is to review changes that were previously made to determine the length of time required to conduct the technical assessment, if there were technical inadequacies (e.g., miscalculated capacities, etc.) in the installed changes, and if there were any systemic failings in the current technical evaluation process. At the end of this phase, a technical evaluation requirements definition end-document is prepared that defines the requirements for conducting a technical evaluation of a change request.

The external design phase for developing the technical evaluation element of the CMM begins by reviewing the technical evaluation requirements definition end-document. The technical objectives of this phase are to determine areas of impact to be analyzed, lead time requirements for conducting a technical evaluation, the meeting requirements for reviewing the status of a technical evaluation, and the criteria for measuring the performance of the technical evaluation process. The internal design focuses on procedures preparing input and output specifications, defining programs or other aids that will be needed to administer a technical evaluation, estimating staff requirements, and outlining the responsibilities and duties of each staff member who will be involved in the conduct of a technical evaluation. When all of the tasks have been completed, a technical evaluation design document should be prepared that establishes the design framework for the technical evaluation element of the change control methodology.

The program and test phases of the technical evaluation element focus on transforming the internal design specifications into physical form structures and finalizing the procedures for conducting the technical evaluation. The tasks involved include the graphics production of the forms, publication of procedures, acquisition of programs and other aids, and completion and testing of any programs required. The deliverables of the construction phase are the procedures, forms, and any tools acquired or developed to assist in the administration of the technical evaluation process.

The tasks involved in implementing the technical evaluation element include scheduling evaluation activities, making any adjustments to the procedures indicated by the test process, and initiating the reporting and performance measurement processes.

Business Evaluation Element. This element of the CMM is concerned with establishing procedures for assessing the business risk, effect, and installation timing of a proposed change.

The requirements definition phase begins by gathering information needed to evaluate existing mechanisms for assessing the business risk of implementing a requested change. The first step is to collect information needed to determine how business plans are channeled to the data processing group, how data processing schedules and plans are channeled to business managers (e.g., operations manager, purchasing manager, accounting manager, etc.), and how the data processing plans are correlated with the business plans. The next step is to analyze the current business evaluation process to determine if it supports the current business objectives and can meet future requirements. At the end of this phase, a business evaluation requirements definition document should be prepared that defines the requirements for conducting a business evaluation of a change request.

The external design phase for developing the business evaluation element of the CMM begins by reviewing the business evaluation requirements definition document. The technical objectives of this phase are to identify the types of changes that will require a business evaluation, define the approach for analyzing the business impact of a requested change, and establish criteria for measuring the performance of the business evaluation process. The internal design phase of developing the business assessment element of the CMM focuses on procedures for preparing input and output specifications, defining programs or other aids that will be needed to administer a business evaluation, estimating staff requirements, and outlining the responsibilities and duties of each staff member who will be involved in the conduct of a business evaluation. When all the tasks have been completed, a business evaluation design document should be prepared that establishes the design framework for the business evaluation element of the change control methodology.

The program and test phases of the business evaluation element focus on transforming the internal design specifications into physical form structures and finalizing the procedures for conducting the business evaluation. The tasks involved include the graphics production of the forms, publication of procedures, acquisition of programs and other aids, and completion and testing of any programs required. The deliverables of the construction phase are the procedures, forms, and any tools acquired or developed to assist in the administration of the business evaluation process.

The tasks involved in implementing the business evaluation element include making any adjustments to the procedures indicated by the test process, and initiating the reporting and performance measurement processes.

Management Review Element. This element of the CMM defines procedures for evaluating the technical and business assessments relative to changes in the configuration identification.

The requirements definition process begins by gathering information needed to evaluate existing mechanisms for assessing the management review process. The first step is to collect information needed to determine how management currently makes go/no-go decisions. This involves reviewing minutes of change management minutes, determining if adequate information is available to support the decision making process, and identifying the types of changes that are subject to management review. The next step is to analyze the current process to evaluate its strengths and weaknesses. The process should culminate with the preparation of a management review requirements definition document that defines the requirements for conducting a management review of a change request.

The external design phase for developing the management review element of the CMM should begin by reviewing the management review requirements definition document. The technical objectives of this phase are to identify the types of changes to be reviewed and the individuals and organizations who will participate in the reviews, and to establish criteria for measuring the effectiveness of the management review process. The internal design phase begins by reviewing the management review external design phase end-document. The first step in the internal design process is to determine the composition of the change control board and to define the functions to be performed by each member of the board. The second step is to prepare procedures for scheduling and conducting the review meetings and for reporting on the actions of the board. The design of several types of documents may be required (e.g., change action reports, discrepancy reports, status reports, etc.). When all the design tasks have been completed, a management review design phase document establishes the design framework for the management review element of the change control methodology.

The program and test phases of the management review element focus on transforming the internal design specifications into physical structures and finalizing the procedures for conducting the management reviews. The tasks involved include the graphics production of the forms, publication of procedures, acquisition of programs and other aids, and completion and testing of any programs required. The deliverables of the construction phase are the procedures, forms, and any tools acquired or developed to assist in the administration of the management review process.

The tasks involved in implementing the management review element include scheduling management review meetings, making any adjustments to the procedures that may recommended by the management review teams, and initiating the reporting and performance measurement processes.

Test Tracking Element. The test tracking element of the CMM focuses on protocols for tracking and documenting test progress and communicating the results to all concerned.

The requirements definition phase begins by gathering information that describes the current procedures for tracking test progress. The first step is to gather information that describes jobstreams that are used for testing and identifies tools and other aids used to facilitate the testing process. The second step is to analyze the current procedures to ascertain if tests were run on all changes or on just select changes and the levels of testing performed. At the end of this phase, a test tracking requirements definition document is prepared that describes the current test tracking procedures and evaluates if the procedures adequately stress the system and the application programs.

The external design phase of developing the test tracking element of the change control methodology begins by reviewing the rest tracking requirements definition document. The technical objectives of this phase are to define a test environment that can simulate the production environment, determine the levels of stress required that should be performed, establish procedures for reporting test results, and identify various test performance indicators (e.g., ratio of outages, number of changes, etc.). The internal design phase begins by reviewing the test tracking external design document. The first sequence of steps in the internal design process focuses on refining the objectives of the test tracking element. The tasks involved include identifying sources of test data, identifying programs and aids that can be used to facilitate the test tracking process, identifying the test participants, and defining their responsibilities. The second sequence of tasks focuses on establishing guidelines for the preparation of test plans, test specifications, test procedures, and test reports. When all of tasks have been completed, a test tracking design document should be prepared that establishes the design framework for the test tracking element of the change control methodology.

The program and test phases of the test tracking element review of the change management methodology element focus on transforming the internal design specifications into physical structures and finalizing the procedures for tracking test results. The tasks involved include the graphics production of the forms, publication of procedures, acquisition of programs and other aids, and creation of the test environment. The deliverables of the construction phase are the procedures, forms, and any tools acquired or developed to assist in the administration of the test tracking process.

The tasks involved in implementing the test tracking element of the change management methodology focus on the publication of procedures that provide step-by-step instructions for scheduling tests, documenting test results, deferring a change based on the test results, and updating change control logs.

Installation Tracking Element. This element of the CMM establishes protocols for tracking and documenting the installation progress of all changes to a baseline identification.

The requirements definition phase begins by gathering information that describes the current procedures for tracking installation progress. The first step is to gather and glean information from documents that describe current hardware and software inventories, provide a history of the changes that have been made to each item in the inventory, and explain how installation problems are detected and resolved. The second step is to analyze the current installation tracking procedures to identify the strengths and weaknesses. At the end of this phase, an installation tracking requirements definition document is prepared that describes the current installation tracking procedures and evaluates if the procedures are adequate.

The external design phase of developing the installation tracking element of the change control methodology begins by reviewing the installation tracking requirements definition document. The technical objective of this phase is to construct a model that shows how the installation tracking element should function. The components of the model should include a master calendar for installing changes; guidelines for processing concurrent changes in the hardware, software, and application environments; and procedures for maintaining logs required to effectively track the change installation process. The internal design phase focuses on procedures for preparing specifications for input and output data flows, status reporting, staffing and scheduling, and verifying that the modified baseline performs effectively in its operating environment. When all the tasks have been completed, an installation tracking design document is prepared that establishes the design framework for the installation tracking element of the change control methodology.

The program and test phases of the installation tracking element of the change management methodology focus on transforming the internal design specifications into physical structures and finalizing the procedures for tracking installation results. The tasks involved include the graphics production of the forms, publication of procedures, the acquisition of programs and other aids, staffing and training, and performing functional tests to ensure the tools or aids are working properly. The deliverables of the construction phase are the procedures, forms, and any tools acquired or developed to assist in the administration of the installation tracking process.

The tasks involved in implementing the installation tracking element focus on ensuring that proper approvals and required preparations have been completed prior to installation. They concentrate on ensuring that adequate time and proper skills are available, inventory records are updated, instructions for installation and backup are completed, and that proper notifications are provided to all concerned parties. In general, the goal is to administer the installation process so that it promotes cooperation, eases resistance, and minimizes backouts and outages. Both successful and unsuccessful installations should be documented.

4.5 Task 5: Prepare Configuration Control Procedures

Formal procedures are required to control changes to the software identification. The established policies for software configuration management define why something must be done, but it is in the context of procedures that explain *what, by whom,* and *when* the work will be performed that the policies are executed. A list of procedures that should be considered in planning and developing a software configuration control system is shown in Table 4-2.

Table 4-2. Software Configuration Control Procedures

Procedure	Objective
Change request	To gain consistency in preparing a change request document and routing the change request to the change control board
Change classification	To gain consistency in classifying changes and prioritizing changes based on urgency
Technical assessment	To ensure the successful integration of the proposed changes by assessing the technical risks that may occur
Business assessment	To ensure that the timing of the proposed change is not disruptive and that the change is compatible with the business goals
Approval procedure	To ensure that only changes that meet the technical and business standards are approved and implemented
Test tracking	To ensure that testing standards are used to create and execute tests plans and that test results are properly communicated
Installation tracking	To ensure that all approved changes have been obtained and that the dates, times and durations of each change activity are properly recorded
Report and control	To ensure that the actions of change control administrators are properly communicated

Change Request Procedure. A procedure should be defined for initiating a request for change that would alter the existing baseline identification. This is accomplished through the use of a change request document that will serve as the vehicle of communications among the various entities involved in effecting the proposed change. The objectives of this procedure are to gain consistency in preparing a change request document and routing it to the change control board for review and approval.

Example:

A. GENERAL
This procedure defines the steps involved in initiating a request for change and communicating the request to all parties involved in the change process. The change request (CR) document is the primary instrument for initiating a change to an existing requirement or limitation of the system. The CR may be initiated by anyone in the user or development organizations and submitted through approved channels to the change control administrators.

B. PROCEDURES

1. Prepare a change request (see attachment C-1)
   Note: A change request is not required to implement a preapproved procedure for backup and recovery.
2. Identify the type of change. (See attachment C-2 for valid change types.)
3. Categorize the change. (See attachment C-3 for valid change categories.)
4. Notify all organizations that may be impacted by the requested change Initiate communications to all organizations impacted by change.
5. Route change request to approvers and reviewers.

C. ATTACHMENTS

Procedure for Classifying and Prioritizing Change Requests. A procedure should be defined for classifying and prioritizing a change request. The objectives of this procedure are to gain consistency in classifying changes that impact the baselines, costs, schedules, and the configuration environment; and prioritizing changes based on urgency.

Example:

A. PROCEDURE FOR CLASSIFYING CHANGES
Change requests shall be classified as either class I or class II. A change is classified Class I when one or more of the following factors are affected by a change to the configuration identification:

- Baseline changes
  - Functional baseline change
  - Allocated baseline change
  - Design baseline change
  - Product baseline change
  - Operational baseline change

- Nontechnical changes
  - Cost change
  - Schedule change

- Environment changes
  - Support hardware change
  - Support software change

- Operation/maintenance manual change

A change to the configuration identification shall be classified class II when it does not fall within the definition of the class I changes noted above.

B. PROCEDURE FOR PRIORITIZING CHANGES
Change requests may also be prioritized as follows:

- Priority Change. This priority is designated when immediate action is required, either because of potential damage to the system or its data base or because a delay in correction might cause significant operational problems.
- Normal Change. This priority is designated when immediate change is not required and normal response times are acceptable.
- Record Change. This priority is designated when corrective action has been taken but concurrence on the change is still required.

Technical Assessment Procedure. A procedure should be defined for evaluating the technical feasibility, technical risk, and technical effect of implementing the change. The objectives of this procedure are to ensure the successful integration of the proposed changes by assessing the technical risks that may occur, determining the levels of testing required, and assessing the installability of the proposed change.

Example:

A. GENERAL
Each change requests shall be subjected to a technical assessment to evaluate the technical feasibility, impact, and risk of the proposed change.

B. PROCEDURE

1. Schedule meetings.
   Responsibility: change coordinator
2. Review history files.
   Responsibility: change coordinator
3. Analyze similar change requests.
   Responsibility: change coordinator, MIS management.
4. Approve, reject, or defer change request.
   Responsibility: MIS management
5. Update appropriate log (i.e., data base change request log, design problem report log, etc.).
   Responsibility: change coordinator
6. Prepare technical assessment report.
   Responsibility: change coordinator
7. Prepare technical assessment report.
   Responsibility: change coordinator
8. Submit report to change control board.
   Responsibility: change coordinator

Business Assessment Procedure. A procedure should be defined for evaluating business risks and the effect based on installation timing. The objectives of this procedure are to ensure that the timing of the proposed change is not disruptive and that the change is compatible with the business goals. The steps and responsibilities involved in conducting a business assessment are the same as the procedures outlined for conducting a technical assessment.

Example:

A. GENERAL
A business assessment shall be made of all proposed changes to a baseline identification. The resulting recommendations will be considered in making determinations to put the change into effect, delay the request, or disapprove the change plan.

B. PROCEDURE

1. Schedule meetings.
   Responsibility: change coordinator
2. Review history files.
   Responsibility: change coordinator
3. Analyze similar change requests.
   Responsibility: change coordinator, MIS management.
4. Approve, reject, or defer change request.
   Responsibility: MIS management
5. Update appropriate log (i.e., data base change request log, design problem report log, etc.).
   Responsibility: change coordinator
6. Prepare technical assessment report.
   Responsibility: change coordinator
7. Prepare technical assessment report.
   Responsibility: change coordinator
8. Submit report to change control board.
   Responsibility: change coordinator

Approval Procedure. The approval process occurs after the technical and business assessments are concluded. A procedure should be defined for evaluating the technical feasibility and business assessments to facilitate the management approval/disapproval process. The objectives of this procedure are to ensure that (1) only changes that meet technical and business standards are approved and implemented and (2) resources are allocated for testing and installing the change into the production environment.

The procedure should define the tasks to be performed and identify the individuals and/or organizational entities who bear responsibility for performing each task.

Example:

A. GENERAL
The approval process shall occur after the technical and business as-

sessments have been completed.

B. PROCEDURE

1. Schedule review and approval meetings.
   Responsibility: change coordinator
2. Conduct approval meeting.
   Responsibility: change coordinator and change control board
3. Prepare appropriate reports
   - Change action report
   - Discrepancy report
   - Discrepancy action report
   - Status report
   Responsibility: change coordinator
4. Prepare schedules for testing and installation.
   Responsibility: MIS management
5. Submit reports to the change initiator and other affected parties.
6. Update appropriate logs (i.e., data base change request log, design problem report log, etc.).
   Responsibility: change coordinator

Test Tracking Procedure. A procedure should be defined for tracking and documenting the test process. The objectives of this procedure are to ensure that testing standards are used to create and execute test plans, test results are communicated to all involved parties, and guidelines are established to evaluate test results.

The procedure should define the tasks to be performed and identify the individuals and/or organizational entities who bear responsibility for performing each task.

Example:

A. GENERAL
All tests must be completed prior to cutover to production.

B. PROCEDURE
The sequence of tasks to be performed is as follows:

1. Verify that all scheduled test have been accomplished.
   Responsibility: change initiator
2. Document all test results.
   Responsibility: change coordinator
3. Approve, disapprove, or defer the change based on the test results.
   Responsibility: MIS manager and/or change control board
4. Update test status log.
   Responsibility: change coordinator

Define Installation Tracking Procedure. A procedure should be defined for tracking and documenting the progress of the installation process. The objectives of this procedure are to ensure that all approved changes have been obtained, the dates, times and durations of each change activity are properly recorded, and proper reports are generated for submission to management.

The procedure should define the tasks to be performed and identify the individuals and/or organizational entities who bear responsibility for performing each task.

Example:

A. GENERAL
To effect a change, the applicable logs and other records must be updated and communicated to all concerned parties.

B. PROCEDURE
The sequence of tasks to be performed is as follows:

1. Notify the change request initiator and all other affected parties that the change is ready for implementation.
   Responsibility: change initiator

2. Schedule and supervise all installation activities.
   Responsibility: change coordinator

3. Update baseline repositories.
   Responsibility: MIS manager and/or change control board

Define Report and Control Procedure. A procedure should be defined to for recording and disseminating:

- The actions of change control administrators
- Discrepancies between the design documents and a program
- The actions or dispositions of discrepancy reports
- Status reports of change requests, change action reports, discrepancy reports, and discrepancy action reports

Examples of reports that may be generated by those concerned with disseminating configuration information include:

- Change action report
- Discrepancy report
- Discrepancy action report
- Status report

The functions of these reports are explained and illustrated on the following pages.

Change Action Report. The change action report is the release document for a CR and serves to record and disseminate the actions of change control administrators. It may also serve as the release form for any supporting reports or studies required by change control administrators to make a proper and informed determination.

Example:

CHANGE ACTION REPORT		
REPORT NO.: ______	CHANGE REQUEST NO.: ______	CHANGE CLASS ☐ I ☐ II

SUBSYSTEM AFFECTED	DOCUMENTATION AFFECTED

STATEMENT OF THE PROBLEM

ACTION REQUIRED

Discrepancy Report. The discrepancy report shall be used to report a discrepancy between the system design document or between the design documents and a program. It contains information on the discrepancy, criticality, recommended priority for change, and any proposed solution or corrective actions taken.

Example:

DISCREPANCY REPORT

REPORT NO.:	CRITICALITY: Priority ______ Normal ______ Record ______

SUBSYSTEM AFFECTED	PROGRAMS AFFECTED	FILES AFFECTED	DOCUMENTATION AFFECTED

REPORTER DATA	ANALYST DATA
Name: ______________________	Name: ______________________
Address: ______________________	Address: ______________________
Phone: ______________________	Phone: ______________________
Date: ______________________	Date: ______________________

DESCRIPTION OF THE DISCREPANCY

Discrepancy Action Report. The discrepancy action report is the release document for a DR. It serves to record the action or disposition on a discrepancy report. The DAR contains specific correction instructions for documentation and programs, together with amplifying information such as an analysis of the discrepancy.

Example:

DISCREPANCY ACTION REPORT

REPORT NO.:________ DR NO.:____________ DATE: __________

ANALYSIS OF DISCREPANCY

ACTION REQUIRED ☐ **Change Request Written** ☐ **No Discrepancy Found**
☐ **Action Described Below Is Required**

ESTIMATED TIME TO ACCOMPLISH ACTION

Status Report. On a periodic basis, change control administrators should publish status reports of outstanding CRs, CARs, DRs, and DARs and should carry an item for at least one reporting period when action on the item has been completed. The project team should provide change control administrators with status information on approved CRs, CARs, DRs, and DARs until completion of system installation.

Example:

STATUS REPORT

SYSTEM____________________ DATE: __________

CR NO.	TITLE	STATUS	COMMENTS

STATUS INDICATORS

P - Decsion Pending
A - CR has been approved
D - CR has been disapproved
X - CR has been deferred by CCB
I - Change has been Installed

4.6 Task 6: Define Methods for Controlling Changes to Baseline Documents

The objective of this task is to define the mechanisms for controlling changes to published baseline documents. The documents describing the system and the procedures for using the system must be changed concurrently with the release of the software modifications. This ensures that errors are not introduced by erroneous instruction or out-of-date specifications. The forms and procedures associated with the document revision control are shown in Figure 4-2.

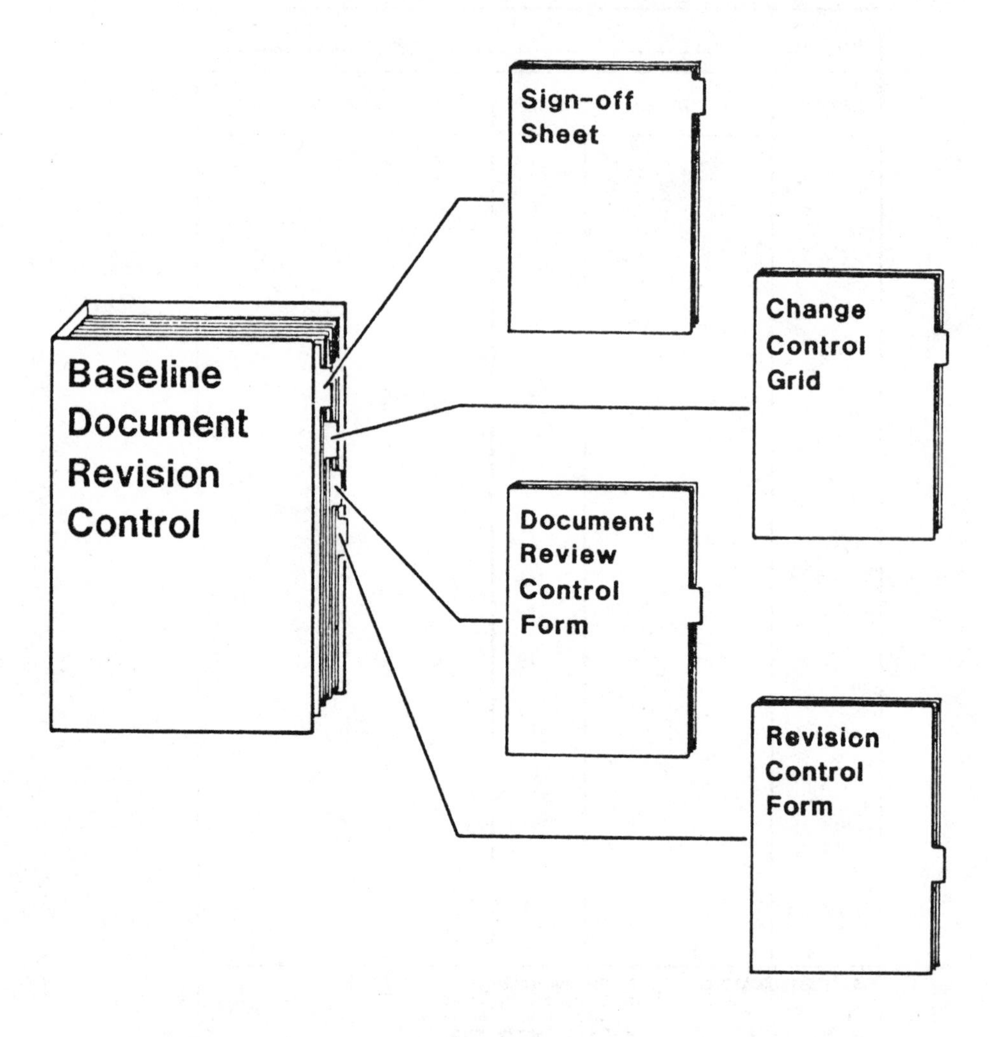

Figure 4-2. Revision Control Documents

Manuscript Review Procedures. The logical step to ensure the accuracy and completeness of baseline documents is to subject the manuscript to formal review prior to publication. The review process starts with providing review copies of the baseline document to the responsible reviewers. The next step is to schedule a conference with the reviewers far enough ahead to allow sufficient time to study the materials. At the review conference, the document should be gone over page by page while questionable points are discussed and changes and corrections noted. When the review conference is concluded, the writer should collect all the review copies and compare them to his/her copy, which was marked during the review. If each reviewer has read and marked his/her copy in advance, the review conference is merely a process of going through the document and resolving the errors. Once the document is officially concurred, the concurrence should be formalized by signing a sign-off sheet. The sign-off sheet should appear as the first page of the baseline document. The review team should include the following:

- MIS manager
- Project team leader
- QA manager
- User manager
- Analyst
- Programmer
- Operations manager

The matrix shown in Figure 4-3 summarizes the review and approval points and the expected participation of project team members in the review process.

	System Requirements Definition	System Design Alternatives	System External Specifications	System Internal Specifications	Program Document	Test Document	Conversion Document	User Guide	Operations Guide
MIS Manager	•	•	•	•	•	•	•	•	•
Project Team Leader	•	•	•	•	•	•	•	•	•
Q A Manager	•	•	•	•	•	•	•	•	•
User Manager	•	•	•			•	•	•	
Analyst	•	•	•	•	•	•	•	•	•
Programmer				•	•	•			
Operations Manager				•		•	•		•

Figure 4-3. Review and Approval Points

Document Status Notations. The status of each baseline document (e.g., first draft, second draft, etc.) should be indicated on the cover of all review copies submitted to reviewers, as shown in Figure 4-4.

ORDER TRACKING SYSTEM
INTERNAL DESIGN

(DESIGN BASELINE DOCUMENT)

Catalog Number
3.2/PC–MIS

FIRST DRAFT

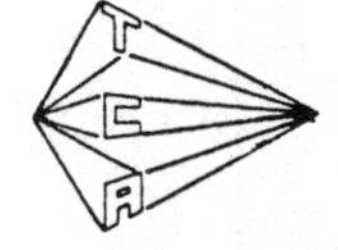

Figure 4-4. Review Copy Status Notation

Document Review Control Form. A document review control form should accompany each copy of a baseline document submitted for review. The form serves as a document log to control the review process. An example of this form is shown in Figure 4-5.

DOCUMENT REVIEW CONTROL FORM

Document Title: ______________________ Catalog Number: __________

____

____

❑ Initial Documentation ❑ Change Documentation ❑ Additions

TRANSMITTAL COMMUNICATIONS

Sent to: ______________________ Date: ______________

Date Requested for Response: ________

Action Required ❑ Acknowledgement of Receipt

❑ Review & Response

❑ Fill in the Gaps of Page/s ____ ____ ____ ____

ACKNOWLEDGMENT OF RECEIPT

Sent to: ______________________ Date: ______________

Tentative Date for Completion of Review: ________

Comments: ______________________________________

ROUTING LIST

Name	Action	By Date

SUMMARY OF RESPONSE

Review Manual Receive From: ______________________________

❑ Corrections/Changes Made as Indicated.

❑ Revised Version Prepared and Resubmitted.

❑ Revised Version Prepared/Document Finalized.

❑ Review Meeting Schedule: ______________

Figure 4-5. Document Review Control Form

Marking Review Copies. Corrections and changes should be neatly made between lines and margins. Professional editing symbols are not generally necessary, but all corrections and changes should be indicated in an orderly manner. An example of corrections penned in by the reviewer is shown in Figure 4-6.

	USER'S GUIDE	**Page:** _______ **Rel. Date:** _______ **Rev. Date:** _______
Section 3.0 - I/O REQUIREMENTS		
3.3 PRODUCTION CONTROL REPORTS (Continued) 3.3.1 PRODUCT/LOCATIONS SUMMARY REPORT (Continued)		
OUTPUT CONTENT		

REF. NO.	COLUMN OR LINE TITLE	DESCRIPTION & INTERPRETATION
14	YLD%	Monthly OUT divided by monthly IN
15	YLD$	Monthly OUT times standard cost
16	LAB	Standard labor cost
17	ITEM NUMBER	THE IDENTIFIER OF AN ITEM. THE KEY TO THE ITEM MASTER FILE.
18	ITEM DESCRIPTION	A DESCRIPTION OF THE ITEM IN THE GENERAL FORM PACKAGE, PDI, CHIP, PRODUCT, MODIFICATION CODE.

Figure 4-6. Example of Marking Review Copies

Conducting the Meeting. When all the documents that establish a baseline have been completed, they should be reviewed to ensure proper identification of configuration items. The person who prepared the baseline document(s) should preside over the review meeting. The meeting itself should be somewhat informal, with the only rules being those of simple courtesy.

Those reviewing the document should focus on its accuracy, not on demonstrating their expertise. The reviewers should keep in mind that the preparer of the baseline document is a human being and is prone to mistakes. They should always use tact when pointing out an error. The writer most likely will appreciate corrections of facts and sloppy grammar. If a different style of writing is suggested other than that prescribed in established standards, the reviewer must direct her/his suggestions to the policymakers rather than to the person who prepared the document.

During the formal review, the document should be systematically reviewed, page by page, while questionable points are discussed and changes and corrections noted. After the formal review, the writer should collect all review copies. Parts of the review copies will probably appear garbled after changes (and changes to changes) have been made, so the writer should transfer the corrections and changes to a previously unmarked copy. As each change or correction is transferred, the writer should read back the sentence or phrase as modified to confirm it has been transferred correctly.

When the review is completed and concurrence and sign-off have been achieved (see the following page), the baseline is considered officially established, as illustrated in Figure 4-7.

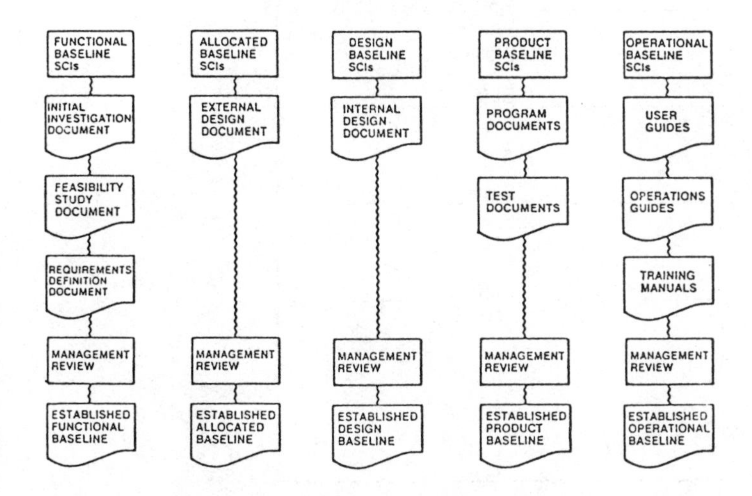

Figure 4-7. Formal Baseline Establishment

Concurrence and Sign-off. Once the reviewers have concurred on the contents of a baseline document, the reviewers should formalize the concurrence by signing a sign-off sheet. This document should be made part of the published work, appearing as the first page of the document. A sample sign-off sheet is shown in Figure 4-8.

DOCUMENT SIGN-OFF

CATALOG NUMBER: ____________________ RELEASE DATE: __________

CUSTOMER SERVICE
USER GUIDE

Approved By: ______________________________ Date ______________

Approved By: ______________________________ Date ______________

Approved By: ______________________________ Date ______________

Approved By: ______________________________ Date ______________

Approved By: ______________________________ Date ______________

Figure 4-8. Example of a Document Sign-off Sheet

Change Control. Changes to baseline documents must be made concurrently with implementation of the change. Formal channels of communications should be established to permit changes to be requested from the users, design and implementation personnel, and operations staff. In a large or complex system, changes may be processed through a change control board.

Since changes are costly in terms of both money and person power, the change system should provide mechanisms for review of dollar costs and approvals of expenditures of any additional funds that may be required.

The flow of processing changes to baseline documents is illustrated in Figure 4-9.

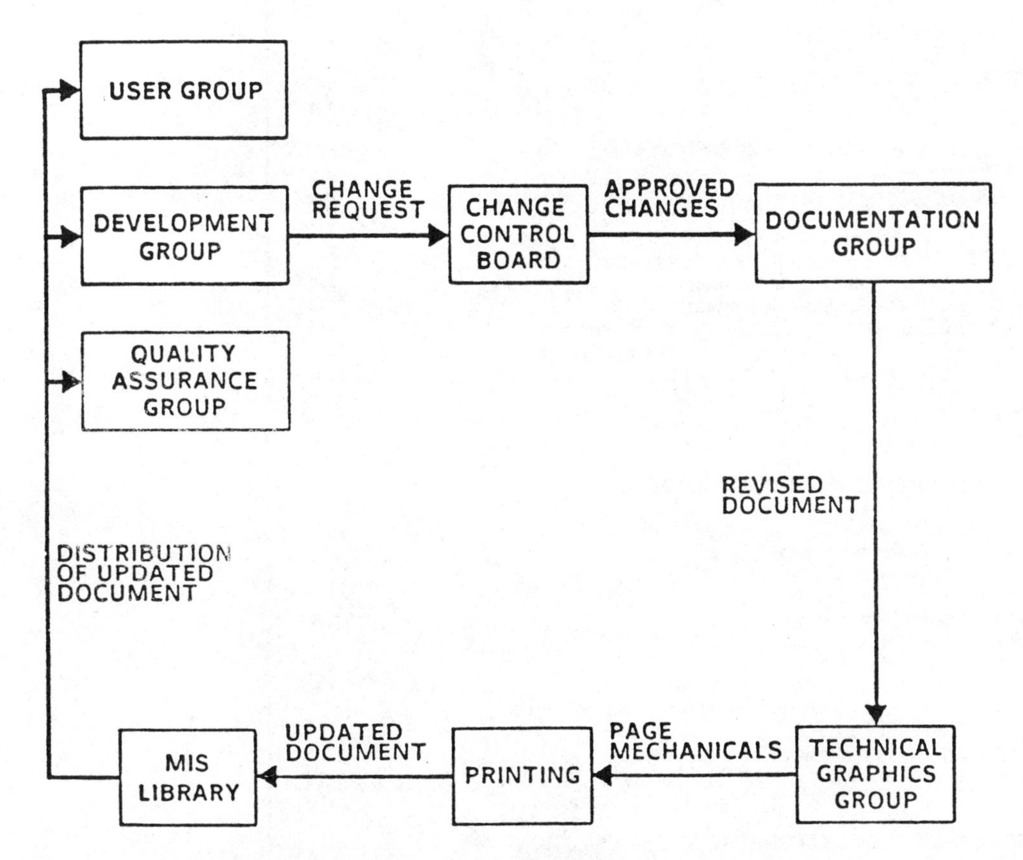

Figure 4-9. Document Change Processing Flow

A number of change control documents may be required to effectively control changes. These include a revision control document and a change control grid. The use of these documents is discussed on the following pages.

Using the Table of Contents as a Checklist. The baseline document table of contents can serve as a checklist for change control by marking the specific sections of the document to be changed. An example is shown in Figure 4-10.

	Equipment Calibration System **PROGRAM DOCUMENT**	Page: ______ Rel. Date: ______ Rev. Date: ______

SECTION 1.0 GENERAL OVERVIEW

SECTION 2.0 PROGRAM DESCRIPTIONS

Add 2.1.9 - EC0070

SECTION 3.0 FILE/RECORD LAYOUTS

SECTION 4.0 PROGRAM CHECKOUT DATA SECTION

Figure 4-10. Example of Using the Table of Contents as a Change Control Checklist

Revision Control Form. Once the changes have been made, the pages to be changed and/or added must be distributed to the holders of baseline documents. A revision control form can be used to instruct the document holders as to which pages to remove from the existing document and which pages to add. An example of a revision control form is shown in Figure 4-11.

	REVISION CONTROL FORM				
Document Title: __________ __________ __________ __________ Catalog Number: ______			Check off revision number on Record of Revision sheet in front of manual Follow REMOVE and FILE Instructions below to update your document.		
REMOVE			FILE		
No.	Pages	Dates	No.	Pages	Dates

Figure 4-11. Example of a Revision Control Form

Change Control Grid. A change control grid may be used to ensure that all corrections and additions that are made at various intervals are included in an end-document. As each change is released, the document holder crosses off the proper revision number on the grid. An example is shown in Figure 4-12.

	System Name: FEASIBILITY STUDY	CHANGE CONTROL GRID

INSTRUCTIONS

(1) Place this revision control grid in front of your document.

(2) Cross off each revision number as revisions are received and filed in your document

	1	2	3	4	5	6	7	8	9	10
	11	12	13	14	15	16	17	18	19	20
	21	22	23	24	25	26	27	28	29	30
	31	32	33	34	35	36	37	38	39	40
	41	42	43	44	45	46	47	48	49	50
	51	52	53	54	55	56	57	58	59	60
	61	62	63	64	65	66	67	68	69	70
	71	72	73	74	75	76	77	78	79	80
	81	82	83	84	85	86	87	88	89	90
	91	92	93	94	95	96	97	98	99	100
	101	102	103	104	105	106	107	108	109	110
	111	112	113	114	115	116	117	118	119	120
	121	122	123	124	125	126	127	128	129	130
	131	132	133	134	135	136	137	138	139	140
	141	142	143	144	145	146	147	148	149	150

Figure 4-12. Change Control Grid

4.7 Summary

Formal procedures are required to control changes to a configuration identification. The major activities that characterize the change management process are change initiation, technical evaluation, business evaluation, management review, test tracking, installation tracking, and formal qualification. In addition, a change coordination activity provides a central point for directing and monitoring the status of each change request.

Configuration policies should be written and published that support the functions of each change processing element. A change initiation policy should be defined to ensure consistency in the way change requests are prepared and submitted for review and approval. Technical and business policies will establish a protocol for evaluating the risk and technical feasibility of a change and ensure that the requested change and timing of the proposed change are compatible with the company's goals. A management review policy will establish a protocol for evaluating the technical and business recommendations. Test tracking and installation policies support the monitoring of test results and installation progress. And a formal qualification policy establishes a protocol for verifying that the modified baseline performs properly in the production environment.

Configuration management standards should be adopted that provide technical and administrative direction for identifying and documenting the functional and physical characteristics of the configuration identification, controlling changes to these characteristics, and recording and reporting change processing and implementation status.

Once policy has defined and the standards for change management have been established, the change management methodology can be designed and developed. Procedures that support the methodology should be defined and promulgated. The methodology should also provide guidance for controlling changes to baseline documents.

Chapter

5

Software Configuration Status Accounting

In this chapter we will consider the fundamentals of *software configuration status accounting* and the procedures used to record and report information needed to manage the software configuration. The focus of the chapter is on the preparation of logs, reports, and version description documents that document the approved configuration identification and report on the status of proposed changes and the implementation of approved changes.

Logs are used to record all activities that impact a configuration item. They create an historical record of the sequence of events that take place from the point of initial release. Logs that may be used to track the status of a configuration item include change request log, problem report log, document update transmittal log, product log, routine log, site installation log, modification report log, specification change notice, and test status log.

Reports are used to inform external parties (i.e., user personnel, management personnel, et al.) of the status of a configuration item. They provide summary information of the status of all change activities during a particular reporting period, specifically the status of change requests, discrepancy reports, problem reports, and tests.

Version description records identify the items delivered and provide information pertaining to editorial changes incorporated since the previous version was released, changes to adaptation data, interfaces affected by the released version, installing and checking out the delivered version, and possible problems and known errors.

It is important to keep in mind as you study this chapter that the focus of software configuration status accounting is on developing a communications system designed to convey relevant information to user and development personnel concerned with the configuration management process.

Thus, the *software configuration accounting* module of the configuration management system serves the following functions: (1) It provides a record of all change actions pertaining to a configuration, (2) it reports on all decisions made and implemented, and (3) It provides a means of storing and cross-referencing the collected data. The tasks involved in developing the configuration management methodology are outlined Figure 5-1.

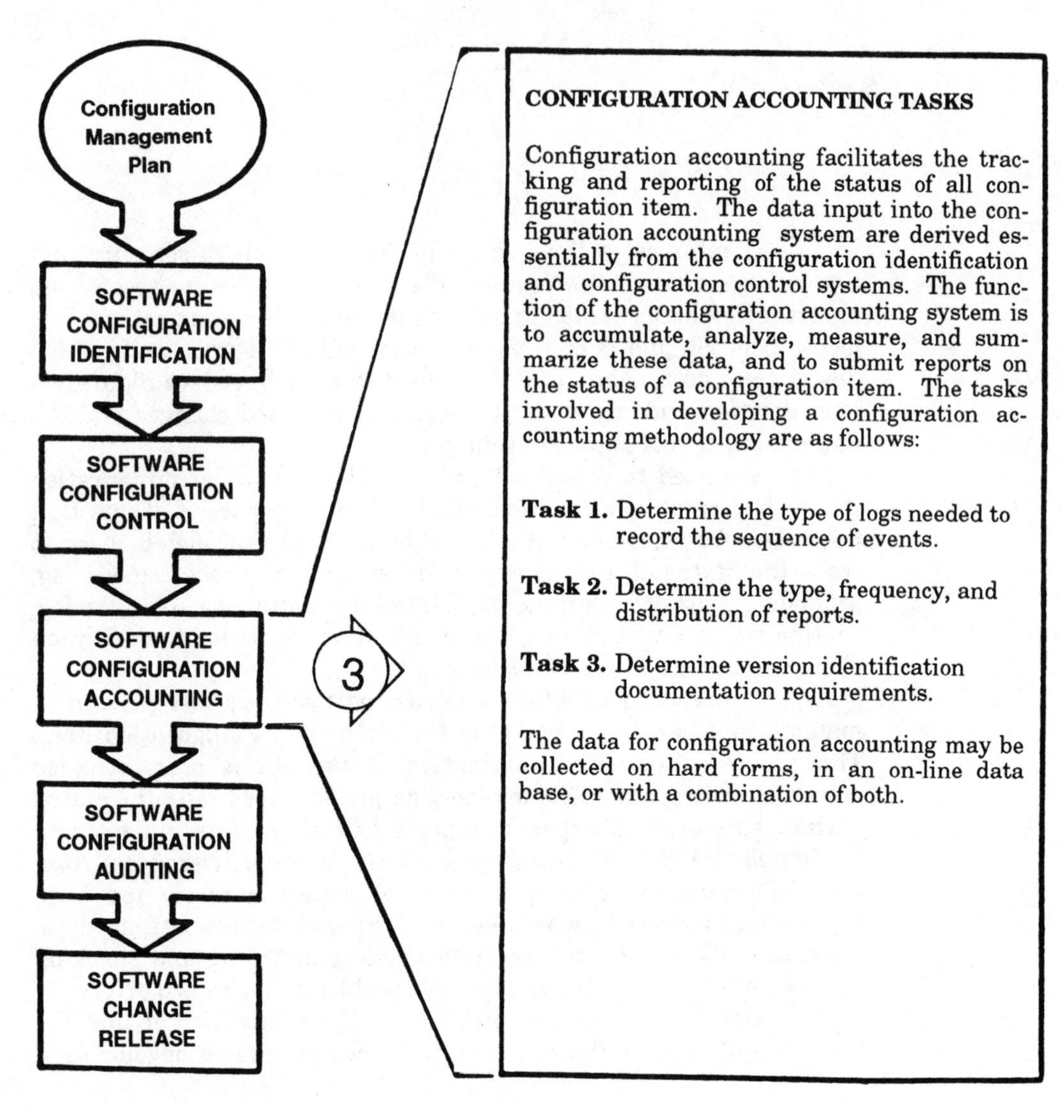

Figure 5-1. Software Configuration Accounting Tasks

The logs used to record the sequence of events that take place from the point of initial release should be designed to:

- Record all activity that impacts the product (i.e., tapes, decks, source listings, object listings, etc.)
- Create an historical record of each routine's development
- List and describe all problem reports, modification records, change notices, and change proposals
- Record installation data

The reports used to inform external parties (i.e., user personnel, management personnel, et al.) of the status of a configuration item should be designed to provide information pertaining to:

- Status of change requests
- Problems detected from the time testing commences through software release
- Status of action taken on problems identified
- Status of a particular program test

The version description records should be designed to provide information pertaining to:

- Editorial changes incorporated since the previous version was released
- Changes to adaptation data
- Interfaces affected by the released version
- Installing and checking out the delivered version
- Possible problems and known errors

After the design of the logs, reports, and version description documents has been completed, the entire software configuration accounting system should be reviewed by the change control board. Upon obtaining the necessary approvals, the CCB should prepare and publish instructions for preparing logs, reports, and version description documents. Adherence to the instruction is mandatory for all user and development personnel involved in the configuration management process. All instructions for preparing the configuration accounting documents should be reviewed periodically to ensure continued applicability and efficiency. When problems or inadequacies are found, revised procedures should be issued.

Software configuration accounting is implemented at the time each baseline identification is approved/accepted. The CCB must ensure that all logs, reports, and version description documents are maintained until the last configuration item is delivered. The specific logs and reports to be prepared should be established by the configuration accounting methodology. The CCB shall bear responsibility for ensuring that there will be a configuration record documenting all approved changes to all software items.

5.1 Task 1: Determine the Type of Logs Needed

Table 5-1 shows a variety of logs that may be used in a configuration accounting system.

Table 5-1. CSA Logs

Log	Ref. Page	Purpose
Data base change request Log	151	Tracks all data base change request data
Design problem report log	152	Lists all design problem reports
Document update transmittal log	153	Lists all document update transmittal forms submitted to the document library
Product log	154	Lists tapes, decks, disks and source listings of all released program configuration items
Routine log	155	Provides an historical record of each routine's development
Site installation log	156	Lists sites where software is installed
Software change proposal log	157	Tracks all software change proposals
Software modification report log	158	Tracks all software modification reports
Software problem report log	159	Lists all software problem reports
Specification change notice log	160	Lists all specification change notices
Test status log	161	Tracks all program testing

Data Base Change Request Log. The function of a data base change request log is to keep track of all data base change request data, including fixes and closure information. The elements of a data base change request log are as follows:

- Identification number of the data base change request
- Name of the person requesting the data base change
- Modification level of the requested data base change
- Location where the data base resides
- Identification number of new version of the data base
- List of user and operator manuals that require revision

A data base change request log is illustrated in Figure 5-2.

DATA BASE CHANGE REQUEST LOG					
DBCR NO.	REQUESTOR	LOCATION	MODIFICATION LEVEL		DOCUMENTS AFFECTED
			Old	New	

Figure 5-2. Data Base Change Request Log

Design Problem Report Log. The function of a design problem report log is to list all design problem reports submitted for change processing. The elements of a design problem report log are:

- The number of the design problem report
- The page and section of the development baseline documents where the problem exists
- The problem category
- Statements of action required
- The closure date for each design problem report

A design problem report log is shown in Figure 5-3.

DESIGN PROBLEM REPORT LOG				
REPORT NUMBER	PAGE/ SECTION	PROBLEM CATEGORY	ACTION REQUIRED	CLOSURE DATE

Figure 5-3. Design Problem Report Log

Document Update Transmittal Log. The function of a document update transmittal log is to list all document update transmittal forms forwarded to the document library or holders of baseline documents that are impacted by changes to configuration items. The elements of this log are:

- The number of the document update transmittal form providing change data;
- The identification number and title of the document to be modified
- The number of the software problem report and software modification report associated with the change.

An example of a document update transmittal log is shown in Figure 5-4.

DOCUMENT UPDATE TRANSMITTAL LOG				
TRANSMITTAL FORM NUMBER	DOCUMENT TO BE MODIFIED		RELATED DOCUMENTS	
	ID	Title	SPR Number	SMR Number

Figure 5-4. Document Update Transmittal Log

Product Log. The function of a product log is to list and describe the tapes, decks, disks and source listings of all released program routines. The elements of a product log include:

- A unique configuration item number
- The item type (e.g., binary, source, print)
- The name and ID number of the program routine
- The modification level of the program routine
- Date of release
- Name of person authorizing the product release
- Library catalog number of the tape, deck, disk, or source listing
- Distribution data showing the number of copies and location of the tapes, decks, source listings, etc.

An example of a product log is shown in Figure 5-5.

PRODUCT LOG										
CONFIGURATION DATA		PROGRAM ROUTINE			RELEASE DATA		LIBRARY CAT. NO.	DISTRIBUTION	
Item No.	Item Type	Name	No.	Mod. Level	Date	Auth.		No.	Location

Figure 5-5. Product Log

Routine Log. A routine is a section of a program or a subprogram that has been isolated for identification. The function of a routine log is to provide an historical record of each routine's development. The basic elements of a Routine Log are:

- Name and identification number of the routine
- Modification number
- List of test cases associated with the software change request
- The number of tape and tape library
- the number of the product specification which established the configuration item
- The ID number of software change proposals for which changes to the configuration item have been made
- The ID number of software change proposals for which changes are still pending

The format and composition of a routine log are illustrated in Figure 5-6.

ROUTINE LOG								
ID NO.	ROUTINE NAME	MOD. NO.	TEST CASES	TAPE NO.	LIB. NO.	SPEC. NO.	SCP NO.	PENDING SCPs

Figure 5-6. Routine Log

Site Installation Log. The function of a site installation log is to identify each site where the software is installed and the software version installed at that site. The components of this log are as follows:

- The identification title and number of the computer program installed
- The date the program was installed
- The location where the program is installed
- The organization authorizing installation

A site installation log is shown in Figure 5-7.

SITE INSTALLATION LOG					
COMPUTER PROGRAM		INSTALLATION ACCOUNTING		VERIFICATION	
Title	ID No.	Date Installed	Location	Auth.	ID No.

Figure 5-7. Site Installation Log

Software Change Proposal Log. The function of a software change proposal log is to track all software change proposals and related software problem reports. The elements of a typical software change proposal log are:

- The number of the software change proposal
- The date the proposal was submitted and logged
- The baseline in which the software change proposal was originated
- The documents affected by the change proposal
- The computer program elements affected by the change proposal

Figure 5-8 illustrates a software change proposal log.

SOFTWARE CHANGE PROPOSAL LOG					
SCP NO.	BASELINE ORIGIN	SUBMISSION DATE	LOG DATE	DOCUMENTS AFFECTED	PROGRAM ELEMENTS AFFECTED

Figure 5-8. Software Change Proposal

Software Modification Report Log. The software modification report log is used to track all software modification reports relating to the configuration items. The data elements of a software modification report log are:

- The software modification report number
- The name of the person who prepared the software modification report
- The associated software problem report number
- The name of the routine(s) affected
- The new modification level number
- The date the report was closed

A software modification report log is shown in Figure 5-9.

SOFTWARE MODIFICATION REPORT LOG

SMR NO.	PREPARED BY	PROBLEM REPORT NO.	ROUTINE NAME	NEW MOD. LEVEL NO.	CLOSE DATE

Figure 5-9. Software Modification Report Log

Software Problem Report Log. The function of a software problem report log is to maintain surveillance of all submitted problem reports. The essential data elements of a software problem report log are:

- Identification number of problem report
- Name of person submitting problem report
- Statement of priority
- Failure analysis category
- Number, date, and type of fix of closure
- Routine modification level
- Number of document update transmittal form that described the changes to be made to documentation

A software problem report log is illustrated in Figure 5-10.

SOFTWARE PROBLEM REPORT LOG								
SPR NO.	SUBMITTED BY	PRIORITY	FAILURE ANALYSIS CATALOG NUMBER	PROBLEM CLOSURE				
				No.	Date	Fix	Mod. Level	Trans. No.

Figure 5-10. Software Problem Report Log

Specification Change Notice Log. The specification change notice log provides a record of all specification change notices. The elements of a specification change notice log are:

- The title of the specification document being changed
- The effective date of revision
- The revision number
- The classification of the software change proposal
- The title and number of the specification and routines affected

An example of a specification change notice log is shown in Figure 5-11.

SPECIFICATION CHANGE NOTICE LOG				
TITLE	REV. DATE	REV. NO.	CHANGE CLASSIFICATION	AFFECTED ROUTINES

Figure 5-11. Specification Change Notice Log

Test Status Log. The function of a test status log is to track the test progress of program unit tests, module integration tests, verification tests, and acceptance tests. The basic elements of a test status log are:

- Name of test
- Test function
- Completion date of test
- Name of data base involved in testing
- New version number of tested software

A test status log is illustrated in Figure 5-12.

TEST STATUS LOG				
TEST NAME	TEST FUNCTION	COMPLETION DATE	DATA BASES	NEW VERSION NUMBER

Figure 5-12. Test Status Log

5.2 Task 2: Determine the Type, Frequency, and Distribution of Reports

Table 5-2 lists a series of reports which may be used to inform external parties (i.e., project team members, user personnel, et al.) of the status of a configuration item.

Table 5-2. Configuration Accounting Reports

Fig. No.	Form Title	Form Purpose
5-13	Change Request Status Summary	Provides summary information of Change Requests submitted during the reporting period.
5-14	Computer Program Inventory	Provides visibility of items in the CPL
5-15	CPL Transmittal Summary Computer program library	Provides summary of data transmitted to the CPL during the reporting period.
5-16	SMR Summary System modification report	Provides summary of SMRs submitted during the reporting period.
5-17	SPR Summary System problem report	Provides summary of SPRs submitted during the reporting period.
5-18	Test Status Summary Report	Provides summary information of tests completed and pending at the time of the report.

Change Request Status Summary. A change request status summary reports the status of all change requests received and logged during a given period. It provides the following information:

- The report number and date of the report
- The numbers and classification IDs of all CRs received during the given period
- The date the CRs were logged
- The actions taken and/or pending on the CRs (i.e., review schedules, change actions, and discrepancy actions)

An example of a change request status summary is shown in Figure 5-13.

CHANGE REQUEST STATUS SUMMARY

REPORT NO.: ______ REPORT DATE: ______

CR NO.	CLASS ID	DATE LOGGED	ACTION				
			Review Scheduled	Review completed	CAR No.	DR No.	DAR No.

LEGEND: CR = Change Request; CAR = Change Action Report; DR = Discrepancy Report; DAR = Discrepancy Action Report

Figure 5-13. Change Request Status Summary

Computer Program Inventory Report. The function of a computer program inventory report is to maintain visibility of the configuration items in the computer program library. The elements of this report are:

- A list of all application programs showing release number and version ID
- A list of all test software showing release number and version ID
- A list of documentation showing release number and version ID
- A list of data base items showing release number and version ID
- A list of all test data on computer-sensible media showing release number and version ID

An example of a computer program inventory report is shown in Figure 5-14.

COMPUTER PROGRAM INVENTORY REPORT							
REPORT NO.:				REPORT DATE:			
APPLICATION PROGRAMS							
SCI NO.	DESCRIPTION	RELEASE NUMBER	VERSION ID	SCI NO.	DESCRIPTION	RELEASE NUMBER	VERSION ID
TEST SOFTWARE							
SCI NO.	DESCRIPTION	RELEASE NUMBER	VERSION ID	SCI NO.	DESCRIPTION	RELEASE NUMBER	VERSION ID
DOCUMENTATION							
SCI NO.	DESCRIPTION	RELEASE NUMBER	VERSION ID	SCI NO.	DESCRIPTION	RELEASE NUMBER	VERSION ID
DATA BASE ITEMS							
SCI NO.	DESCRIPTION	RELEASE NUMBER	VERSION ID	SCI NO.	DESCRIPTION	RELEASE NUMBER	VERSION ID
TEST DATA FILES							
SCI NO.	DESCRIPTION	RELEASE NUMBER	VERSION ID	SCI NO.	DESCRIPTION	RELEASE NUMBER	VERSION ID

Figure 5-14. Computer Program Inventory Report

Computer Program Library Transmittal Summary. The function of a computer program library transmittal summary is to report on the transmittal forms logged and the subsequent actions taken during the reporting period. The content of this form includes:

- The identification number of the program, document, or test case being transmitted to the CPL
- The identification number of the transmittal form
- The date of transmittal
- The index number of the base version
- The index number of the new version
- Identification of related software problem reports (SPRs)
- Identification of related software modification reports (SMRs)

An example of a computer program library Transmittal Summary is shown in Figure 5-15.

COMPUTER PROGRAM LIBRARY TRANSMITTAL SUMMARY

REPORT NO.: ______ REPORT DATE: ______

SCI NUMBER	TRANSMITTAL FORM NO.	TRANSMITTAL DATE	CPL DATA			RELATED DOCUMENTS	
			CPL CAT. NO.	RELEASE DATE	VERSION ID	SPR NO.	SMR NO.

LEGEND: SPR = Software Problem Report
SMR = Software Modification Report

Figure 5-15. Computer Program Library Transmittal Summary

Software Modification Report Summary. A software modification report summary is used for reporting actions taken on SMRs received during a specified period. A software modification report summary should include the following information:

- The report number and date
- The SCI Number;
- The SMR number and date; and
- The actions taken and/or pending on the SMRs as follows:
  - Date the report was logged;
  - Date the modification was implemented
  - Associated discrepancy or change request.

Figure 5-16 shows an example of a software modification report summary.

SOFTWARE MODIFICATION REPORT SUMMARY					
REPORT NO.:			REPORT DATE:		
SCI NUMBER	SMR NUMBER	SMR DATE	ACTION		
			DATE LOGGED	DATE IMPLEMENTED	DR/DAR NUMBER
LEGEND: DR = Discrepancy Report DAR = Discrepancy Action Report					

Figure 5-16. Software Modification Report Summary

Software Problem Report Summary. The function of the software problem report summary is to report on the status reports received and the action taken on the reported problems during a specified period.

An example of a software problem report summary is shown in Figure 5-17.

SOFTWARE PROBLEM REPORT SUMMARY					
REPORT NO.: ______			REPORT DATE: ______		
SCI NUMBER	SPR NUMBER	SPR DATE	ACTION		
			DATE LOGGED	DATE IMPLEMENTED	DR/DAR NUMBER
LEGEND: DR = Discrepancy Report DAR = Discrepancy Action Report					

Figure 5-17. Software Problem Report Summary

Test Status Summary Report. The function of the test status summary report is to summarize the status of all program tests. The test status summary report should include the following data:

- The report number and date
- The names of the tests completed
- The result (passed/not passed) of tests run
- The tests still to be run
- The schedule status of the various tests

An example of a test status summary report is shown in Figure 5-18.

TEST STATUS SUMMARY REPORT			
REPORT NO.: ______		REPORT DATE: ______	
TESTS RUN	TEST RESULT	TESTS PENDING	SCHEDULED TEST DATE

Figure 5-18. Test Status Summary Report

5.3 Task 3: Determine Version Identification Documentation Requirements

A *version description document* should be prepared to accompany the release of each version of a computer program configuration item. It should also accompany the release of an interim change (i.e., changes that occur between versions of a computer program configuration item). The version description document should identify all the items delivered and record all pertinent data relating to status and use of the computer program configuration item or change. The content arrangement of a version description document is illustrated in Figure 5-19.

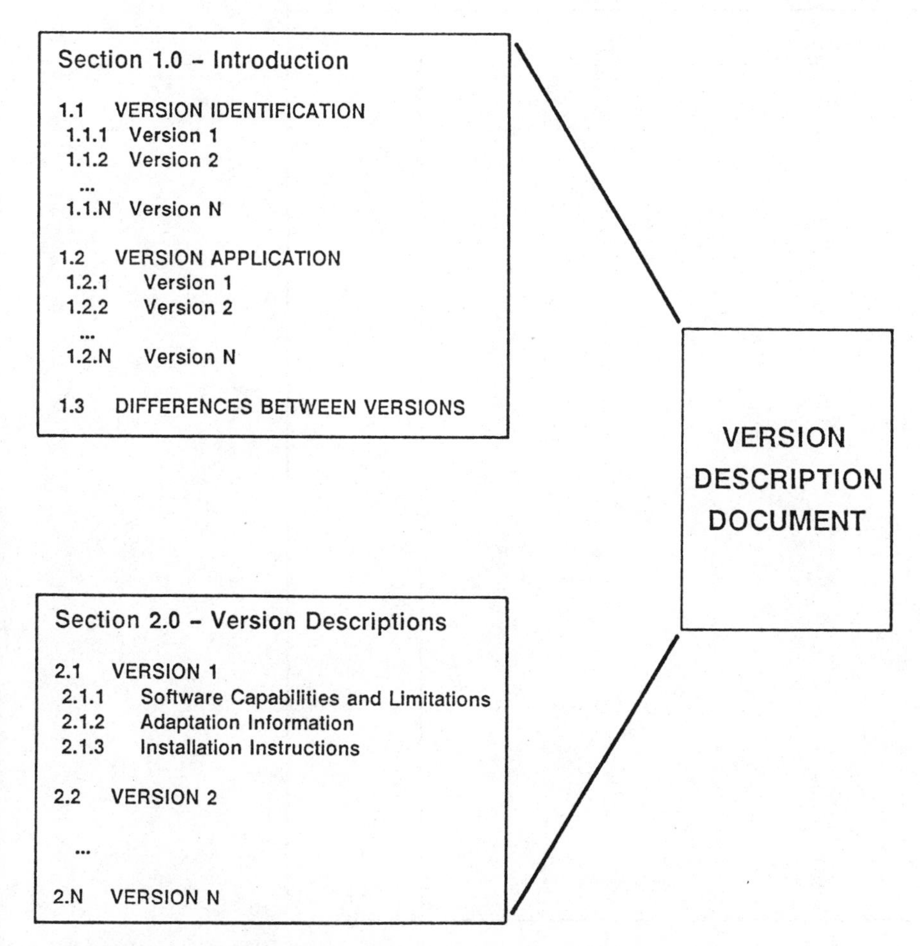

Figure 5-19. Content Arrangement of a Version Description Document

Version Identification Form. The configuration identification for each version and for the delivery media may be recorded on a prestructured form as shown in Figure 5-20.

VERSION DESCRIPTION DOCUMENT		
Section 1.0 - Introduction		
1.1 VERSION IDENTIFICATION 1.1 Version 1		
SCI No.	Description	Media

Figure 5-20. Version Identification Form

Version Application Form. Figure 5-21 shows a prestructured form that was designed to describe the application of the version and to identify superseded versions and other versions still in use.

VERSION DESCRIPTION DOCUMENT	
Section 1.0 – Introduction	
1.2 VERSION APPLICATION 1.2.1 Version 1	
Purpose:	
Superseded Versions	Other Current Versions

Figure 5-21. Version Application Form

Differences-between-Versions Form. The form shown in Figure 5-22 provides a matrix for documenting the differences between the versions of the SCI.

VERSION DESCRIPTION DOCUMENT

Section 1.0 – Introduction

1.3 DIFFERENCES BETWEEN VERSIONS

Function	Version 1	Version 2	Version 3	Version 4	Version 5
Function A	Yes	Yes	No	No	No
Function B	No	Yes	No	Yes	Yes
Function C	Yes	Yes	No	Yes	No
Function D	No	Yes	Yes	Yes	No
etc.					

Figure 5-22. Differences-between-Versions Form

Software Capabilities and Limitations Form. The prestructured form shown in Figure 5-23 is intended to summarize the limitations on software operations imposed by the changes and the capabilities of the version documented.

VERSION DESCRIPTION DOCUMENT
Section 2.0 – Version Descriptions
2.1 VERSION 1 2.1.1 Software Capabilities and Limitiations
Functional Capabilities:
Performance Capabilities:
Limitations/Known Problems:

Figure 5-23. Software Capabilities and Limitations Form

Adaptation Information Form. Figure 5-24 shows a prestructured form that is used to record the changes required to adapt the equipment, operations, or system use to the new version.

VERSION DESCRIPTION DOCUMENT
Section 2.0 - Version Descriptions
2.1 VERSION 1 2.1.2 Adaptation Information
Equipment:
Operational:
Interface:

Figure 5-24. Adaptation Information Form

Installation Instructions Form. The form shown in Figure 5-25 may be used to outline the procedures for installing the software version in the operational environment.

VERSION DESCRIPTION DOCUMENT
Section 2.0 – Version Descriptions
2.1 VERSION 1 2.1.3 Installation Instructions
Library Setup:
Data Base Loading:
System Initiation:

Figure 5-25. Installation Instructions Form

5.4 Summary

Configuration status accounting serves the following functions: (1) It provides a record of all change actions pertaining to a configuration item; (2) it reports on all decisions made and implemented; and (3) it provides a means of storing and cross-referencing the collected data. The vehicles for communications include *logs, reports,* and *version description documents*.

Logs are used to record all activity that impacts a software identification and to create an historical record of each change activity. The logs list and describe all problem reports, modification records, change notices, and change proposals.

Reports are used to inform external parties of the status of a configuration item. They provide information pertaining to the status of change requests, problems detected from the time testing commences through software release, the status of action taken on problems identified, and the status of a particular program test.

Version description records identify the items delivered and provide information pertaining to changes incorporated since the previous version was released. It also identifies interfaces affected by the released version, explains how to install and check out the delivered version, and describes possible problems and known errors.

Chapter

6

Software Configuration Auditing

Configuration auditing is an important function of the configuration management process. Its purpose is to verify and validate that the configuration item (CI) has achieved the performance specified in its baseline identification and that the documentation is adequate for a move to production. Primarily this function involves evaluating test results to verify that the functional requirements have been met and that the CI conforms to the prescribed quality standards. In carrying out this function, the auditor analyzes the test results and relates them to the established test/performance criteria. Additionally, the auditor is responsible for verifying that the CI is compatible with the data base, program, and interface control specifications. The magnitude of these responsibilities may be appreciated when it is realized that a typical computer system is made up of literally thousands of CIs. The auditor, of course, does not examine every level of CIs; rather she or he utilizes professional approaches to ascertain that they were properly measured and reported.

The verification and validation process involves three separate audit functions:

1. *Functional configuration audit* (FCA). The objective of the FCA is to verify that all tests for a configuration item have been completed and that the software performance, based on the test results, meets the specification performance requirements set forth in functional and allocated baseline documents.
2. *Physical configuration audit (PCA).* The objective of the PCA is to verify the adequacy, completeness, and accuracy of the docu-

mentation which establishes a baseline.

3. Formal qualification review (FQR). The function of the FQR is to verify that the configuration item performs in its operating environment.

The complete auditing process is illustrated below in Figure 6-1.

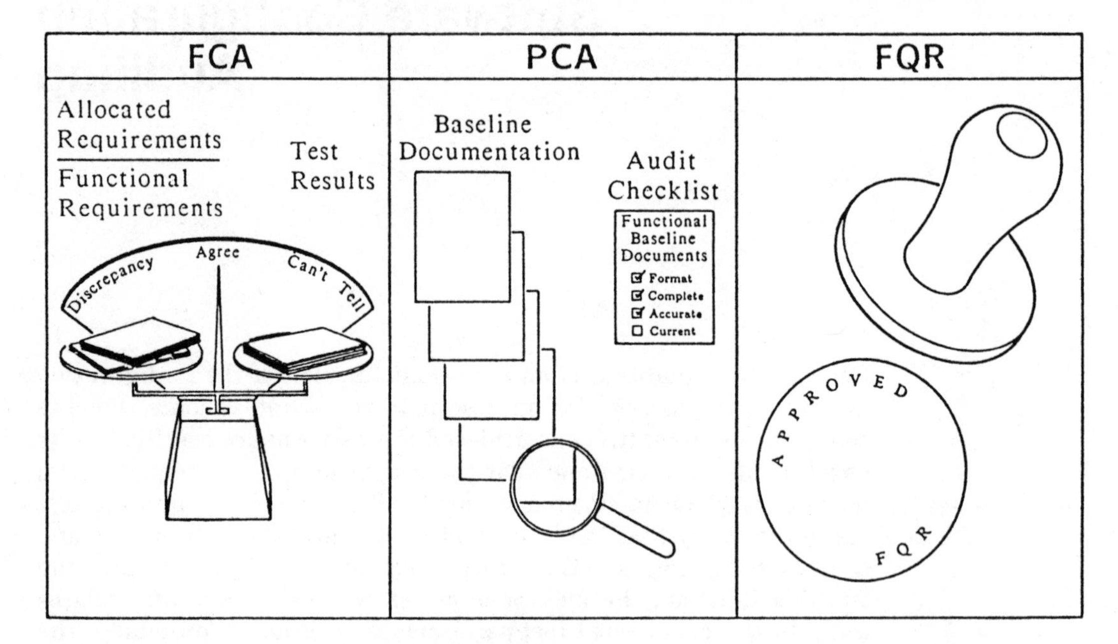

Figure 6-1. Configuration Auditing Process

6.1 Functional Configuration Audit

The FCA encompasses two major functions:

1. It verifies that all unit tests specified in the test plan have been completed.
2. It verifies that the software configuration item (SCI), based on test results, meets the functional and allocated requirements.

In conducting the FCA, the auditor utilizes working papers consisting of the following:

- Checklists
- Questionnaires
- Verification forms
- Configuration audit records

These working papers provide a means for recording and evaluating the evidence collected during the FCA. The functions of each type of working paper are as follows:

Checklists. Checklists of all the functional and allocated performance requirements should be prepared prior to initiating the FCA. These checklists are used in analyzing test reports to determine if the configuration item established at the product baseline meets the requirements defined at the functional and allocated baselines.

Questionnaires. The auditor may interview user and development personnel to further determine the degree to which the requirements have been satisfied. To facilitate the interview process, the auditor may prepare questionnaires that list the questions to be asked in gathering information about performance problems and requirements.

Verification Forms. Forms which allow the auditor to record the results of each audit step can also facilitate the FCA process. The form's design should be sufficiently clear and self-explanatory to enable the auditor to verify the configuration item without resorting to additional data.

Configuration Audit Record. The configuration audit record provides information on the status of the FCA, PCA, and FQR. The record is initiated by the FCA and kept up to date through the FQR. The record includes:

- The number and name of the configuration item audited
- The start and complete dates of the FCA
- The start and complete dates of the PCA
- The FQR certification date

6.1.1 Configuration Auditing Checklists

Configuration auditing checklists provide a framework for conducting audits in an organized and consistent manner. They are prepared to ensure that the auditor does not overlook the important considerations and the salient points that make the difference between a well conducted comprehensive audit and a mediocre audit. The checklists are used in analyzing test reports to determine if the CI established in the product baseline meets the requirements that were defined at the functional, allocated, and design baselines. Several types of checklists may be required to facilitate the FCA. These include:

- Functional requirements checklist

- Allocated requirements checklist
- Configuration item test checklist

The checklists should be prepared prior to initiating the FCA. They may be accompanied with background explanations that explain why certain auditing tasks are applicable.

The use of checklists in planning the FCA is illustrated in Figure 6-2.

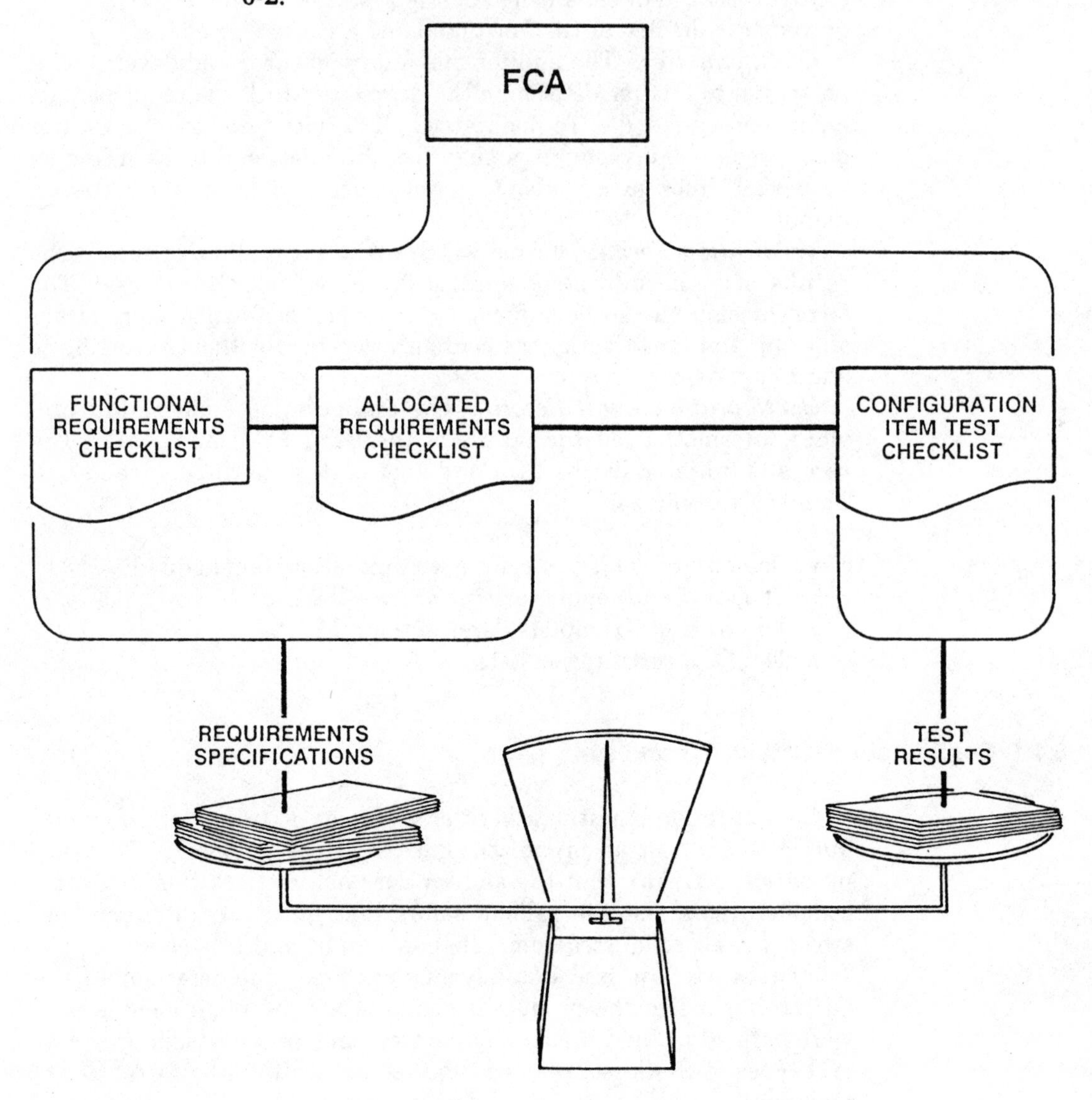

Figure 6-2. FCA Checklists

Functional Requirements Checklist. This checklist identifies all the functional requirements that must be satisfied and references the appropriate specification. An example of a functional requirements checklist is shown in Figure 6-3.

FUNCTIONAL REQUIREMENTS CHECKLIST				
SPEC. NO.	SPECIFICATION	AUDITING FACTORS		
		PERFORMANCE REQUIREMENTS	ENVIRONMENT REQUIREMENTS	DATA REQUIREMENTS
2.1	ACCURACY AND VALIDITY	X		
2.2	TIMING	X		
2.3.1	Backup	X		
2.3.2	Fallback	X		
2.3.3	Restart	X		
3.1	EQUIPMENT ENVIRONMENT			
3.1.1	Processors		X	
3.1.2	Storage Media		X	
3.1.3	Input Device(s)		X	
3.1.4	Communications		X	
3.2	SUPPORT SOFTWARE ENVIRONMENT		X	
3.2.1	Support Software		X	
3.2.2	Input & Equipment Simulators		X	
3.2.3	Test Software		X	
3.2.4	Utilities		X	
3.2.5	Operating System		X	
3.2.6	Data Management System		X	
3.3	INTERFACES		X	
3.4	SECURITY AND PRIVACY		X	
3.5	CONTROL REQUIREMENTS		X	
4.1	DATA DESCRIPTION			
4.1.1	Static System Data			X
4.1.2	Dynamic Input Data			X
4.1.3	Dynamic Output Data			X
4.2	DATA COLLECTION REQUIREMENTS			X
4.3	INPUT FORMATS			X
4.4	OUTPUT FORMATS			X
4.5	DATA BASE IMPACTS			X
4.5.1	Equipment Impacts			X
4.5.2	Software Impacts			X
4.5.3	Organizational Impacts			X
4.5.4	Development Impacts			X

Figure 6-3. Functional Requirements Checklist

Allocated Requirements Checklist. This checklist identifies all requirements allocated to the system software and hardware. An example of an allocated requirements checklist is shown in Figure 6-4.

ALLOCATED REQUIREMENTS CHECKLIST

SPEC. NO.	SPECIFICATION	AUDITING FACTORS			
		SYS/SUBSYS ALLOCATION	SECURITY & CONTROL REQ	TECH ENVIRON-MENT REQ	INTERFACING REQ
2.1	SYSTEM SCHEMATIC	X			
2.2	SYSTEM FUNCTIONS	X			
2.3	SYSTEM INPUT DATA				
2.3.1	Source Documents	X			
2.3.2	Record/Transaction Content	X			
2.3.3	Table Contents	X			
2.3.4	File Contents	X			
2.3.5	Inputs From Other Systems	X			
2.4	PROCESSING LOGIC				
2.4.1	Input Processing Logic	X			
2.4.2	Data Base/File Processing Logic	X			
2.4.3	History File Processing Logic	X			
2.4.4	Table Processing Logic	X			
2.4.5	Output Processing Logic	X			
2.5	OUTPUT DESCRIPTIONS	X			
2.5.1	Output Document Formats	X			
2.5.2	Output Screen Formats	X			
3.1	SECURITY AND PRIVACY		X		
3.2	CONTROLS		X		
4.1	HARDWARE CONSIDERATIONS				
4.1.1	CPU			X	
4.1.2	Storage			X	
4.1.3	Communications			X	
4.1.4	Terminals			X	
4.2	SOFTWARE CONSIDERATIONS				
4.2.1	Data Base			X	
4.2.2	Teleprocessing			X	
4.2.3	Programming Language			X	
4.3	PERFORMANCE CRITERIA				
4.3.1	Acceptable Response Time			X	
4.3.2	System Update Window			X	
5.1	HARDWARE INTERFACES				
5.1.1	Interface Equipment				X
5.1.2	Operational Implications				X
5.2	SOFTWARE INTERFACES				
5.2.1	Type of Interface				X
5.2.2	Operational Implications				X
5.2.3	Data Transfer Requirements				X
5.2.4	Current Formats				X
5.2.5	Interface Procedures				X

Figure 6-4. Allocated Requirements Checklist

Configuration Item Test Checklist. This checklist itemizes all the major test activities which are considered in testing if the current status of a configuration item meets the specified functional and allocated requirements. Figure 6-5 provides an example of a configuration item test checklist.

CONFIGURATION ITEM TEST CHECKLIST			
SPEC NO.	TEST LEVEL	FUNCTION TESTED	SCIs AFFECTED (Spec Number)
1.1.1	Unit	Processing Logic Routine 1	AB 2/4/2
2.1.1	Integration	Processing Logic Routine 1	AB 2/4/2
3.1.1	System	Processing Logic Routine 1	AB 2/4/2
1.1.2	Unit	Processing Logic Routine 2	AB 2/4/2
2.1.2	Integration	Processing Logic Routine 2	AB 2/4/2
3.1.2	System	Processing Logic Routine 2	AB 2/4/2
1.1.3	Unit	Processing Logic Routine 3	AB 2/4/2
2.1.3	Integration	Processing Logic Routine 3	AB 2/4/2
3.1.3	System	Processing Logic Routine 3	AB 2/4/2
1.2.1	Unit	Input Processing Logic	AB 2/4/1
2.2.1	Integration	Input Processing Logic	AB 2/4/1
3.2.1	System	Input Processing Logic	AB 2/4/1
1.3.1	Unit	History Processing Logic A	AB 2/4/3
2.3.1	Integration	History Processing Logic A	AB 2/4/3
3.3.1	System	History Processing Logic A	AB 2/4/3
1.3.2	Unit	History Processing Logic B	AB 2/4/3
2.3.2	Integration	History Processing Logic B	AB 2/4/3
3.3.2	System	History Processing Logic B	AB 1/4/3
1.3.3	Unit	History Processing Logic C	AB 2/4/3
2.3.3	Integration	History Processing Logic C	AB 2/4/3
3.3.3	System	History Processing Logic C	AB 2/4/3
1.4.1	Unit	Table Processing Logic 1	AB 2/4/5
2.4.1	Integration	Table Processing Logic 1	AB 2/4/5
3.4.1	System	Table Processing Logic 1	AB 2/4/5
1.4.2	Unit	Table Processing Logic 2	AB 2/4/5
2.4.2	Integration	Table Processing Logic 2	AB 2/4/5
3.4.2	System	Table Processing Logic 2	AB 2/4/5

Figure 6-5. Configuration Item Test Checklist

6.1.2 Questionnaires

Before conducting interviews, the auditor must determine what data is to be gathered from the interview. To facilitate the process, interview questionnaires should be developed which can be used as a guide. During the interview, the auditor may record the responses to the questions on an interview worksheet which references the questions by number and also allows for additional questions to be added pursuant to the interview responses. Finally, the results of the interview are analyzed, and a synopsis of the findings are presented in an interview summary. There are three main forms associated with the questionnaire process:

- Questionnaire form
- Interview worksheet
- Interview summary

The steps involved in the interview process are graphically illustrated in Figure 6-6. The content of each form associated with the questionnaire process is discussed and illustrated on the follow pages.

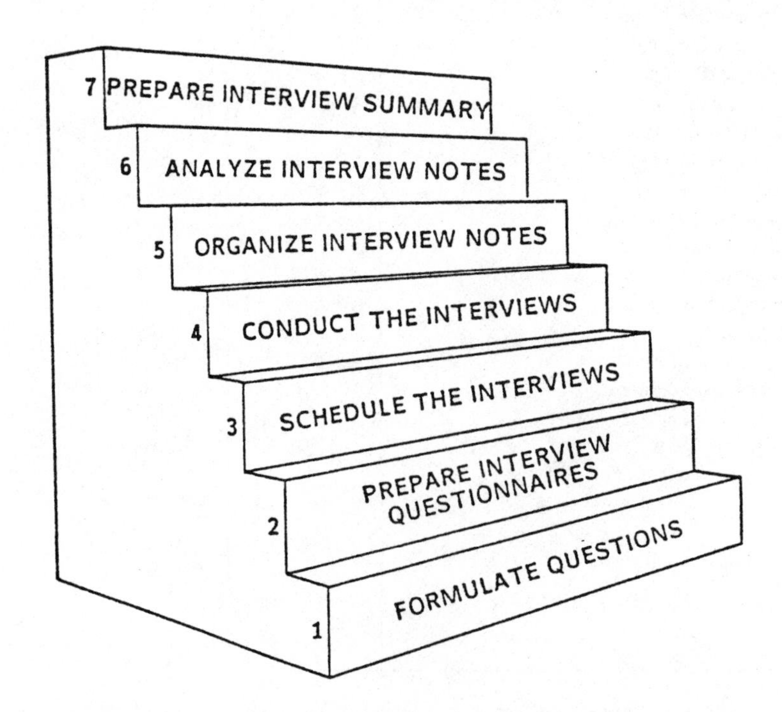

Figure 6-6. Interview Process

Interview Questionnaires. The elements of a questionnaire form may include:

- Question numbers (i.e., a unique number should be assigned to each question)
- Specific questions to be asked
- Name of person(s) to be interviewed

An example of an auditing questionnaire form is shown in Figure 6-7.

FCA QUESTIONNAIRE

QUESTION NUMBER	REFERENCE SPEC	QUESTION	INTERVIEWEE
1	FB 2.1	Are there accuracy and validity requirements beyond those specified in section 2.1 of the functional baseline?	
2	FB 2.2	Are there timing requirements agreed upon, but undocumented in the functional baseline document?	
3	FB 2.3	Are there failure requirements agreed upon but undocumented in the functional baseline document?	
4	FB 2	Does the installed system meet the requirements as specified?	
5	FB 3.1	Do the equipment specifications in the functional baseline reflect all of the actual requirements?	
6	FB 3.3	Were the interface requirements for gathering data completely satisfied?	

Figure 6-7. Auditing Questionnaire Form

Interview Worksheet. The interview worksheet provides an important source of information to assist the auditor in deciding on the appropriate audit report. The elements of this form may be as follows:

- Referenced question number
- Name of the person interviewed
- Interviewees response

An example of an interview worksheet is shown in Figure 6-8.

FCA AUDIT INTERVIEW WORKSHEET		
QUESTION NUMBER	REFERENCE	Interviewee: ________________
1	Yes	
1.1	(What were they?) The calculation of interest payable must be double checked against actuals during month-end closings to validate the model.	
1.2	(Why weren't these incorporated in the specs?) The interest payment calculation was added after the original spec was written and when it was added, the validity requirements were added in a verbal agreement.	
2	No	
3	Yes - But must confirm with C. Dalton in Purchasing	
4		
etc.		

Figure 6-8. Interview Worksheet

Interview Summary. In addition to the interview worksheets, the auditor may prepare interview summaries that are maintained as permanent working papers. This approach enables the auditor to summarize in one place the essence of the information gathered from the interviews. The elements of an interview summary form may be as follows:

- Reference question number
- Respondent's identification/initials
- Response summary

An example of an interview summary form is shown in Figure 6-9.

FCA INTERVIEW SUMMARIES		
QUESTION NUMBER	RESPONDENT'S INITIALS	RESPONSE SUMMARIES
1	JD	There is one validity check incorporated in the requirements. That check is that the interest calculation in the forecasting model be checked against actual data during the month-end closing. It is incorporated into the system but left from the specification as an oversight.
2	JD	The specification incorporates all timing requirements
3	JD	Refer question to C. Dalton
etc		etc

Figure 6-9. Interview Summary Form

6.1.3 Verification Forms

As previously stated, the function of an FCA is to verify that the test results for a configuration item coincide with the functional and allocated requirements. This means that the auditor must carefully evaluate the test/performance criteria in order to verify that the test results satisfy the functional and allocated requirements.

Utilizing the functional and allocated checklists (see pages 181-182) and the configuration item test checklist (see page 183), the auditor proceeds to verify that tests have been completed for each requirement. In addition, the auditor must review the test results to verify that the tests adequately demonstrated that the system requirements were met.

Three forms that may be used by the auditor to assist the verification process are:

- Accuracy and validity verification form
- Data integrity verification form
- Performance verification form

Figure 6-10 demonstrates the verification process.

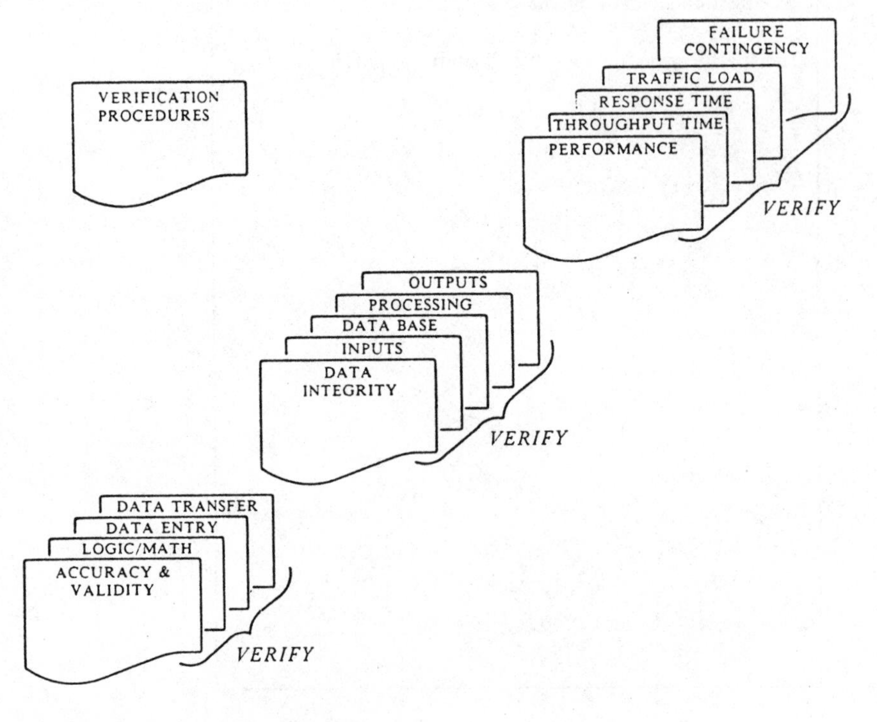

Figure 6-10. Verification Process

Accuracy and Validity Verification Form. An Accuracy and validity verification form may be used to verify the accuracy and validity of the current status of a configuration item. The elements of this form may be as follows:

- Name and number of the configuration item being verified
- Date of verification
- Name of the auditor verifying the configuration item
- Reference to logic/math requirements specification
- Reference to data requirements specification
- Reference to data transfer requirements specification
- Auditor's findings (i.e., agreement, deficiency, insufficient data, etc.)

An example of an accuracy and validity verification form is shown in Figure 6-11.

FUNCTIONAL REQUIREMENTS CHECKLIST

Configuration Item: Date Verified:
No.: By:

SPEC. NO.	LOGIC/MATH REQUIREMENTS	DATA ENTRY REQUIREMENTS	DATA TRANSFER REQUIREMENTS	TEST RESULTS		
				Agrees	Discrepancy	Insuff. Data

Figure 6-11. Accuracy and Validity Verification Form

Data Integrity Verification Form. The auditor may use a data integrity verification Form to summarize the data integrity audit factors. The elements of this form may be as follows:

- Name and number of the configuration item being verified
- Date of verification
- Name of the auditor verifying the configuration item
- Number identification of applicable requirements specification
- Configuration item input identification
- Configuration item data base identification
- Configuration item processing identification
- Configuration item output identification
- Auditor's findings (i.e., agreement, discrepancy, insufficient data, etc.)

An example of a data integrity verification Form is shown in Figure 6-12.

DATA INTEGRITY VERIFICATION FORM

Configuration Item: Date Verified:
No.: By:

SPEC. NO.	INPUTS	DATA BASE	PROCESSING	OUTPUTS	TEST RESULTS		
					Agrees	Discrepancy	Insuff. Data

Figure 6-12. Data Integrity Verification Form

Performance Verification Form. The auditor may use a performance verification form to summarize the performance audit factors. The elements of this form may be as follows:

- Name and number of the configuration item being verified
- Date of verification
- Name of the auditor verifying the configuration item
- Number identification of applicable requirements specification
- Throughput time test number
- Response time test number
- Traffic load test number
- Auditor's findings (i.e., agreement, deficiency, insufficient data, etc.)

An example of a performance verification form is shown in Figure 6-13.

FUNCTIONAL REQUIREMENTS CHECKLIST

Configuration item: Date Verified:
No.: By:

SPEC. NO.	THROUGHPUT TIME TEST NO.	RESPONSE TIME TEST NO.	TRAFFIC LOAD TEST NO.	TEST RESULTS		
				Agrees	Discrepancy	Insuff. Data

Figure 6-13. Performance Verification Form

6.2 Physical Configuration Audit

The Physical configuration audit is conducted to verify the adequacy and accuracy of the documentation that establishes the product baseline for a software configuration item. The PCA is accomplished by establishing the compatibility of the configuration item to be qualified to the following released documentation:

- Design documentation
- Test documentation
- Version description documentation
- Change control documentation

The review of design documentation enables the auditor to verify the correlation of a configuration item to the data base, program, and interface control specifications.

The PCA establishes the validity of production acceptance testing by comparing the test data with the SCI's specified performance requirements.

The identification markings and numbers for computer program SCIs are compared with the version description document.

Program package configuration items such as program listings, object listings, and cross-references are compared to change control documentation to verify that all approved changes have been incorporated. The software release system and change control procedures themselves should be reviewed and validated to verify that they comply with established standards.

The design and test specifications, once audited, will serve as the basic documentation for acceptance requirements and specification control of all subsequent changes and modifications to a configuration item.

Normally, only one PCA is accomplished for an SCI. However, if a major software change occurs or the auditor finds that the configuration item for which a PCA is performed does not accurately reflect the released documentation, the complete PCA may be conducted again.

Checklists should be prepared to assist the auditor in comparing an SCI to the design, test, version description, and change control documentation. The design and application of such checklists are discussed and illustrated on the following pages.

6.2.1 Design Documentation Checklist

The purpose of the design documentation checklist is to verify the adequacy, accuracy, and completeness of the documentation that defines the data bases, master files, and work files that must be established. An example of a design documentation checklist is shown in Figure 6-14.

DESIGN DOCUMENTATION CHECKLIST			
SCI	DOCUMENTATION STATUS		
	Complete	Current	Accurate
GENERAL			
Project References			
Index of Programs			
Index of Files			
Index of Outputs			
INPUTS AND OUTPUTS			
Input Document Formats			
Input Screen Formats			
Output Document Formats			
Output Screen Formats			
DATA BASE SPECIFICATIONS			
Data Base Summary			
Labeling/Tagging Conventions			
Data Base Organization			
Special Instructions			
File Layouts			
Table Layouts			
Record Layouts			
PROGRAM SPECIFICATIONS			
Support Software Environments			
Interfaces			
Storage Requirements			
Program Design			
- Detail Summary			
- Logic Flow			
- Initialization/Sign-on			
- Operator Messages			
- User Messages			
- Job Setup			
CONTROLS AND SECURITY			
I/O Controls			
User Controls			
Data Base/File Controls			
Access Controls			
Error Controls			
Audit Trails			
BACKUP/RECOVERY			
Backup Procedures			
File Retention Procedures			
Restart Procedures			

Figure 6-14. Design Documentation Checklist

6.2.2 Test Documentation Checklist

The purpose of the test documentation checklist is to verify the adequacy, accuracy, and completeness of the documentation that defines the test specifications and test evaluation procedures. Figure 6-15 provides an example of a test documentation checklist.

TEST DOCUMENTATION CHECKLIST			
SCI	DOCUMENTATION STATUS		
	Complete	Current	Accurate
COMPUTER PROGRAM TEST PLAN			
Testing Requirements			
Test Management Requirements			
Personnel Requirements			
Hardware Requirements			
Supporting Software Requirements			
Schedule			
Quality Assurance			
COMPUTER PROGRAM TEST SPECIFICATIONS			
Testing Requirements			
Test Management Requirements			
Personnel Requirements			
Hardware Requirements			
Supporting Software Requirements			
Schedule			
Quality Assurance			
COMPUTER PROGRAM TEST PROCEDURES			
Testing Requirements			
Test Management Requirements			
Personnel Requirements			
Hardware Requirements			
Supporting Software Requirements			
Schedule			
Quality Assurance			
COMPUTER PROGRAM TEST REPORT			
Test Results			
Evaluation Criteria			
Test Evaluation			
Recommendations			

Figure 6-15. Test Documentation Checklist

6.2.3 Version Description Documentation Checklist

The purpose of the version description documentation checklist is to verify the adequacy, accuracy, and completeness of the documentation that identifies the current version and describes the version capabilities. An example of a version description documentation checklist is shown in Figure 6-16.

VERSION DESCRIPTION DOCUMENTATION CHECKLIST			
SCI	DOCUMENTATION STATUS		
	Complete	Current	Accurate
VERSION 1			
Change Summary			
Limitations			
Adaptation Information			
Interface Compatibility			
Changes			
Installation Instructions			
VERSION 2			
Change Summary			
Limitations			
Adaptation Information			
Interface Compatibility			
Changes			
Installation Instructions			
VERSION 3			
Change Summary			
Limitations			
Adaptation Information			
Interface Compatibility			
Changes			
Installation Instructions			
VERSION 4			
Change Summary			
Limitations			
Adaptation Information			
Interface Compatibility			
Changes			
Installation Instructions			

Figure 6-16. Version Description Documentation Checklist

6.2.4 Change Control Documentation Checklist

The purpose of the change control documentation checklist is to verify the adequacy, accuracy, and completeness of the logs and status reports that are used to monitor changes to a configuration item. An example of a change control documentation checklist is shown in Figure 6-17.

CHANGE CONTROL DOCUMENTATION CHECKLIST			
SCI	DOCUMENTATION STATUS		
	Complete	Current	Accurate
CHANGE CLASSIFICATION INDEX			
CHANGE REQUESTS			
CHANGE ACTION REPORT			
DISCREPANCY REPORT			
DISCREPANCY ACTION REPORT			
STATUS REPORT			

Figure 6-17. Change Control Documentation Checklist

6.3 FORMAL QUALIFICATION REVIEW

A formal qualification review is conducted to establish that the SCI performs in its operating environment. This is accomplished through an incremental review of test data. The review establishes that all required tests have been completed and that the software configuration item performs as required.

If the FQR determines that the tested SCI performs in accord with the specification requirements, the SCI is certified and the date of certification entered on a configuration item development record. The FQR process is depicted in Figure 6-18.

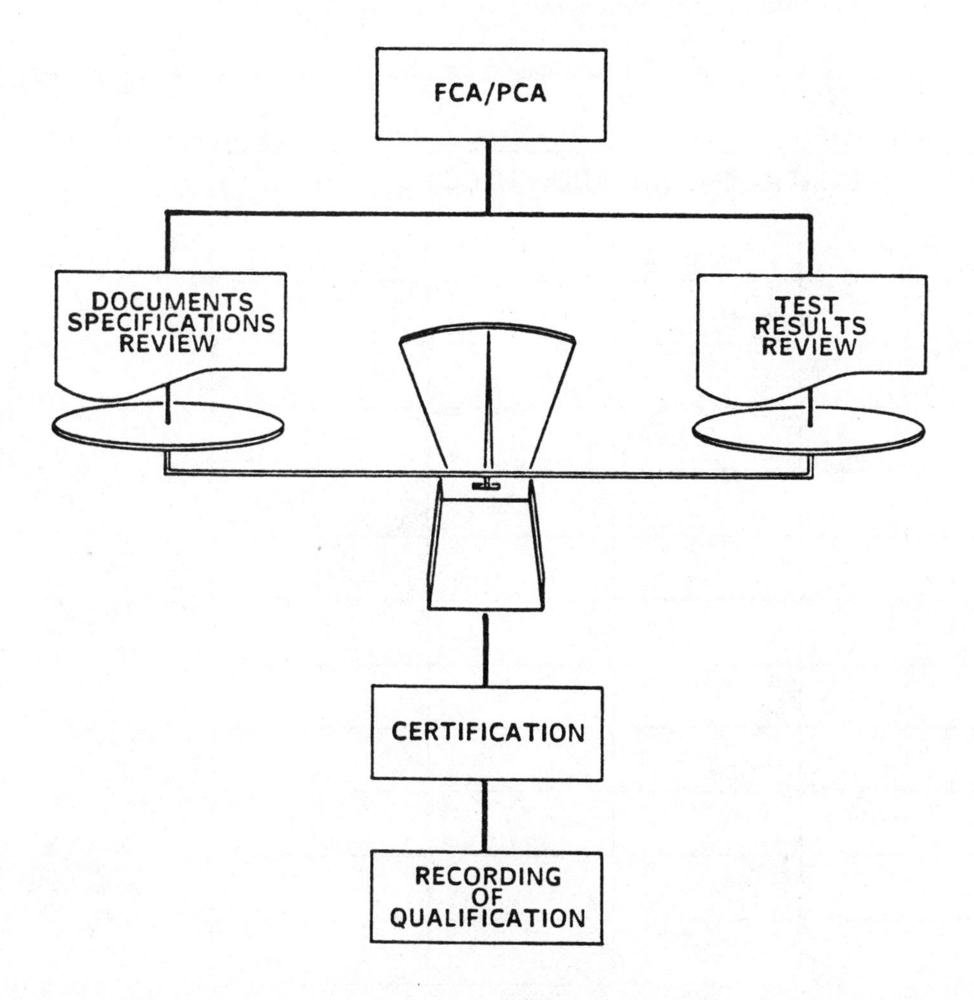

Figure 6-18. Formal Qualification Review Process

6.3.1 Configuration Audit Record

The configuration audit record provides status information on the development progress of the SCI as determined by the FCA, PCA, and FQR processes. Each configuration audit record contains information which may be included in the configuration status accounting system. The elements of the configuration audit record are as follows:

- Number and name of the SCI
- Start and complete date of the FCA
- Start and complete date of the PCA
- FQR certification date

An example of a configuration audit record is shown in Figure 6-19.

CONFIGURATION AUDIT RECORD				
SCI NO.	SCI NAME	FCA	PCA	FQR
		Start: Complete:	Start: Complete:	Date Certified

Figure 6-19. Configuration Audit Record

6.4 SUMMARY

Configuration management audits should be conducted periodically to ensure that policies and procedures are being met.

A *functional configuration audit* should be conducted to verify that all unit tests specified in the test plan have been completed and that the configuration item, based on test results, meets the functional and allocated requirements. In conducting the FCA, the auditor utilizes working papers consisting of checklists, questionnaires, verification forms and configuration audit records. These working papers provide a means for recording and evaluating the evidence collected during the FCA.

A *physical configuration audit* is conducted to verify the adequacy and accuracy of the documentation that establishes the product baseline for configuration management. The PCA is accomplished by establishing the compatibility of the configuration item to be qualified to the design and test documentation. The design and test specifications, when validated, serve as the basic documentation for acceptance requirements and specification control of all subsequent changes and modifications to a configuration item.

A *formal qualification review* is conducted to establish that the SCI performs in its operating environment. If the FQR determines that the tested configuration item performs in accord with the specification requirements, the item is certified and the date of certification entered on a configuration item development record.

Glossary

Acceptance Testing
The series of tests designed to demonstrate the functional capabilities of a software configuration item.

Allocate
To assign functional requirements to main routines and subroutines.

Allocated Baseline
The baseline that evaluates design alternatives, defines the system/subsystem functions, explains the system data and processing logic, and allocates functional requirements to specified routines and programs.

Analysis
The methodical investigation of a problem and the separation of the problem into smaller related units for further study.

Approval/Validation
The official authorization that is granted to a software configuration item to be placed into the operational environment.

Baseline
A set of configuration items resulting from the tasks performed during specific phases of the software development process. The baseline defines the configuration identification at a specified point in the development cycle. (*See also* Functional baseline, Allocated baseline, Design baseline, Product baseline, and Operational baseline.)

Business Evaluation
The process of ensuring that the requested change and the timing of the proposed change are compatible with the organization's goals.

Change Control Board (CCB)
The coordinating entity that provides central direction for the processing of changes to a configuration baseline.

Change Initiation
The process of requesting changes to configuration items for which identification has been established.

Configuration
The aggregate of deliverable items that result from the tasks performed during the phased development of a computer system.

Configuration Accounting
The process of recording and reporting information needed in the management of the software configuration.

Configuration Audit
The process of verifying and validating that the physical and functional configuration matches the documented baseline identification.

Configuration Control
The process of systematically evaluating, coordinating, approving or disapproving, and implementing changes to the baseline configuration identification.

Configuration Identification
The technical documentation that describes or defines an aggregation of software or any of its discrete portions that satisfies an end-user function and for which separate configuration records must be maintained.

Configuration Item
Either the aggregation of the elements that comprise a specific deliverable or a subset of the configuration identification.

Design Baseline
The baseline that provides the specifications programmers need to code the modules, including input/output specifications, data base specifications, program specifications, security and control specifications, backup specifications, testing and implementation plans, and summaries and cross-references.

Deliverable
The record of accomplishment that describes the results of each task

performed during the phased development of a computer system.

End Document
The vehicle of communication that cumulates and arranges the phase deliverables for presentation in a published manual.

External Design
The phase of software development that establishes specifications that divide the system into subsystems and define the subsystem interfaces and the development and operational priorities.

Feasibility Study
The phase of software development that compares the present system to the proposed system and identifies probable costs and consequences.

Formal Qualification
A protocol for verifying that the modified baseline performs properly in a production environment.

Functional Baseline
The baseline that defines the problem and need, projects costs and target schedules, analyzes the present and proposed systems, and specifies the functional requirements of a proposed system.

Initial Investigation
The phase of software development that addresses the potential of the proposed system relative to cost and benefits.

Installation Tracking
The process of monitoring the installation progress of all changes to configuration items.

Internal Design
The phase of software development that establishes specifications for data bases, master files, and work files; specify required hardware and software configurations; explain how to modify software packages; and provide the specifications programmers need to code the programs.

Labeling Scheme
The method for uniquely identifying each software configuration item.

Management
The administrative discipline that is exercised to identify and document the functional and physical requirements of each software configuration item, control changes to those characteristics, record and report change processing and implementation status, and verify and validate software performance and the adequacy and completeness of documentation.

Management Review
The process of evaluating the technical and business recommendations and approving or disapproving a change request.

Operational Baseline
The baseline established by implementation documents such as the operating program code, conversion documents, user guides, operations guides, and training manuals.

Product Baseline
The baseline established by documentation that includes program performance and design specifications, program description documents, program package documents, test plans, test specifications, test procedures, and test reports.

Programming
The process of transforming the design specification into executable code.

Requirements Definition
The phase of software development that defines the functional requirements for the proposed system, identifies the types and frequencies of inputs and outputs, describes the required data bases or files, establishes system controls, and explains the required interfaces.

Software
The programs, procedures, routines, and all documents associated with the analysis, design, programming, conversion, and implementation of a computer system.

Software Configuration Management
The process of identifying, tracking, and controlling changes to software configuration items.

Software Configuration Management Plan
The document that defines the policies and procedures to be followed

in exercising administrative surveillance in identifying, tracking, and controlling changes to software configuration items.

Systems Development Methodology
A set of mutually supportive and integrated guidelines organized into a series of chronological phases that make up the development cycle of a computer system.

Technical Evaluation
The process of evaluating the risk and technical feasibility of implementing a change request.

Testing
The process of verifying that the program performs as specified in the design and requirements specifications.

Test Tracking
The process of monitoring test results and test progress.

Validation
The performance of tests and evaluations to determine compliance with the functional and technical requirements.

Verification
The process of determining if a configuration identification supports or contradicts the functional or technical requirements.

Version
A program product identified by a version number indicating the enhancements contained in a particular offering of a software product.

Index

ABOUT THE AUTHORS

Steve Ayer and Frank S. Patrinostro (Sunnyvale, Calif.) are founders of Technical Communications Associates. Frank S. Patrinostro, recognized worldwide as a documentation specialist, has served as a consultant to government and industry for over 20 years. Steve Ayer has worked as a documentation specialist and methods analyst for several of the nation's leading companies, including ITT, Fairchild, and Westinghouse. He conducts numerous seminars (mostly on-site) on how to document a computer system. They have both authored several works on documentation development and management, including the excellent companion volume to this book: Ayer and Patrinostro's *Documenting the Software Development Process*.